Bathrooms

Bathrooms

CREATING THE PERFECT BATHING EXPERIENCE

Vinny Lee

jacqui
small

First published in 2007 by Jacqui Small LLP,
an imprint of Aurum Books Ltd,
25 Bedford Avenue, London WC1B 3AT

Text copyright © Vinny Lee 2007
Photography, design and layout copyright
© Jacqui Small 2007

The author's moral rights have been asserted.

All rights reserved. No part of this book may
be reproduced, stored in a retrieval system or
transmitted, in any form or by any means,
electronic, electrostatic, magnetic tape,
mechanical, photocopying, recording or
otherwise, without prior permission in
writing from the publisher.

PUBLISHER Jacqui Small
EDITORIAL MANAGER Kate John
DESIGNER Maggie Town
EDITOR Hilary Mandleberg
PICTURE RESEARCHER Nadine Bazar
PRODUCTION Peter Colley

ISBN 978 1 903221 70 9

A catalogue record for this book is available
from the British Library.

2009 2008 2007
10 9 8 7 6 5 4 3 2 1

Printed in China

contents

Bathrooms are now so much more than just a space in which to wash; they are a focal point of the twenty-first-century home – a place where style matters, designer labels are to be found and cutting-edge technology is in action. What is more, they now concentrate just as much on caring for and conditioning the inner self as the outer self.

Most modern homes have more than one bathroom. The most desirable configuration is an en-suite shower room for a quick and efficient cleanse in the morning, and a separate, larger and more indulgent room with a bath and enough space to pamper yourself, relax and unwind. In some apartments, the bathroom may not even contain a bath. Instead, you are as likely to find a hammam-style combination steam and shower cabinet or a Japanese-inspired cedar-wood plunge tub as the centre of attention.

Yet bathrooms are still, basically, utilitarian spaces that have a unique mix of demands, technological requirement and safety specification. These 'wet' spaces need careful planning, budgeting, co-ordinating and, above all, expert installation so they function efficiently, utilise hi-tech developments effectively and still manage to look effortlessly inviting.

Vinny Lee

OPPOSITE TOP Details such as staggered shelves with coloured glass vases and bottles provide not only a screen in front of the window but add colour and interest to a simple bathroom scheme.

OPPOSITE BELOW Organic shapes and smooth outlines feature in many contemporary bathrooms.

THIS PAGE A linear scheme with the bath and shower along one wall maximises the space.

OVERLEAF In this roof-space bathroom there is scope for a pair of basins on a generously sized countertop as well as a bath that does not have to hug the wall.

Planning

In bathroom planning, size matters — it will dictate the proportions and quantity of bathroom fittings and furniture that you can install. Ergonomics — the study of the efficient use of space and how people work within it — are also important because a bathroom needs to be a place that operates smoothly and efficiently as well as being somewhere that is safe and relaxing.

TOP LEFT A band of contrasting tiles near the top of the wall helps to add height to a room, which is a useful trick in a small or boxy space. The same goes for using light-reflecting glazed white tiles.

TOP RIGHT It is important to evaluate, with the help of a professional plumber, how to achieve access to pipes, waste and water supplies. A large proportion of any bathroom design budget goes on the 'invisible' plumbing and electrical work that is concealed behind tiles and facings.

BOTTOM LEFT Marry up the style of basin or bath you choose with the décor of the room and its location. In this African setting with plastered walls, ventilation is important to avoid the walls becoming damp.

BOTTOM RIGHT When planning where to put things in a small bathroom make sure that the access is clear and unobstructed and that the opening and closing of the door will not impinge on the use of the basin, bath or toilet.

In a small bathroom keep the number of different items you include to a minimum and opt for smaller rather than grand-scale choices. In a large bathroom you can afford a more generously sized bath and a basin with a surround, but align them carefully so that it is still easy to move around — especially if more than one person uses the bathroom at the same time.

It isn't only the floor space that needs to be analysed but also the relationship between items. For instance, avoid putting a hand basin directly beside or over the toilet or bidet, so that you don't bang your head or shoulder against the basin rim when getting up or down.

When planning storage, calculate the distance needed to open cupboard doors and, if space is limited, try sliding panels or a curtain instead. In a small cloakroom consider whether a tall person will be able to sit down and close the door comfortably. Such trivial-sounding considerations are important to the overall design and use of any bathroom or cloakroom space.

WHAT DO YOU NEED?

ABOVE An additional basin for brushing teeth and washing hands and face can take the pressure off a main bathroom.

ABOVE RIGHT By concealing the toilet cistern, the appearance of the bathroom is much cleaner and less cluttered.

OPPOSITE If space is at a premium a shower over a bath provides two types of washing in one place.

When you first start to plan your bathroom, the question to ask yourself is what do you and your household need from this room? To help gauge this, it can be useful to think about the following: How many of you are there in the household? How much time does each person need in the bathroom and at what time of day? Do you prefer to take baths or showers, or do you like to start the day with a quick, invigorating shower and end it with a relaxing bath before going to bed? Are 'extras' such as a sauna or steam room on your wish-list? Must your bathroom or toilet cater for children, the elderly or visitors?

If you are a working couple, both of whom need to get ready in the morning and leave home at roughly the same time, avoiding hold-ups and frayed nerves in the bathroom is most likely to be your aim. Is it a matter of staggering your timing or is there space for you to double up in the

LEFT A moveable step is an ideal way to cater for people of various heights or for children and adults using the same bathroom.

RIGHT Having two basins speeds up washing and getting-ready time for a couple in the morning and at bedtime, but also means that toiletries can't always be kept exactly where they will be used.

BELOW A glass panel separates the walk-in shower from the toilet and the handle doubles as a useful towel rail.

bathroom, perhaps by reconfiguring the room to accommodate a second hand basin so that the two can be used simultaneously? Or could a second toilet and basin be plumbed in elsewhere in the home so that the bathroom becomes the principal washing zone and there is secondary back-up?

If you are a family household with children getting ready for school at the same time as the adults are preparing to leave for work, can you have a main family bathroom and find space for an en suite for the parents? Failing that, might there be room for a separate toilet and wash basin to complement the family bathroom? Alternatively, it might be possible to avoid having a single all-purpose bathroom and instead have smaller ancillary spaces such as a shower room or wet room, plus a separate toilet and wash basin. Whichever permutation you choose, the idea is to disperse the workload of the main bathroom to ease the pressure and make morning rush less stressful.

INDIVIDUAL NEEDS

What you require in the way of bathroom and toilet facilities will vary according to the composition of your household and the configuration of your home. The needs of a family with babies or toddlers, or of one with

LEFT Here a mosaic-tiled partition screens off the toilet area while providing a handy surface to which a shower and the shower curtain can be fixed.

RIGHT A large bathroom can be sub-divided down the centre, placing the bath on one side of the freestanding wall while accommodating a basin and storage on the other. If these fixtures were placed in a linear arrangement along the side walls, the room would appear vast and empty.

elderly people are different from those of a childless professional couple, and they will also be different if your home is on several storeys. If you live in a house on two or three floors and have a young child at toilet-training stage, or elderly relatives with impaired mobility, you ideally need a toilet and hand basin on every floor, or at least one on the ground floor for daytime use.

A ground-floor cloakroom–toilet is also useful for guests or casual visitors who you may not want to have walking through your home or going into your personal bathroom space. It will also save on muddy shoes trailing through halls and up staircases to reach a bathroom on an upper floor.

If you can only accommodate one bath-type space, have a wet room with a hand-held or adjustable shower head as well as static nozzles. Wet rooms are easy to access, even by wheelchair, and the build-up of heat and moisture can be therapeutic and relaxing. A seat or bench will allow an elderly, injured or infirm person to sit down and wash, rather than having to stand.

DIVIDING THE SPACE

In a large bathroom, the use of partitions and panels
to divide up the space not only contributes to the décor and style of the room
but also makes the space more versatile. The most obvious reason to divide
the space is to screen off the lavatory and provide some privacy. Another
reason is to create a room within a room so the bath, for example, can be in its
own quiet, self-contained space. Or you may simply want to stop splashes
from a shower going all over the floor.

Various materials can be used to construct freestanding walls, partitions
or panels, depending on the effect you are trying to achieve and the purpose
for which the division is intended. For the most solid-looking walls, the best
option is a stud-partition faced with plasterboard. This can be floor-to-ceiling
or half-height and can be finished with tiling, paint or plaster. In the most

OPPOSITE LEFT A random pattern of tiles makes the partition separating the toilet and basin area almost invisible against the far wall as well as contributing to the overall decoration of the room.

OPPOSITE RIGHT A panel or dividing wall can have a sculptural appearance. Here, a gently sloping upper edge gives a softer, more attractive outline.

THIS PAGE Glass is widely used to make bathroom walls and enclosures because it is waterproof and allows the light through.

LEFT A dual-purpose panel separates the bath from the basin but also provides a useful mirror directly in front of the basin.

ABOVE As in a wet room, this shower has no enclosure or curtain and a drainage outlet in the floor channels the water away.

ABOVE RIGHT Looking from the shower to the other side of the room, you can see that the dual-purpose panel is the same size and shape as the wall-mounted cupboard.

modern, design-led interiors these walls are often sculpturally curved in semi-circles or sensuous S-shapes (see pages 68–71).

If you decide to have a natural plaster finish, the surface should be finished with an appropriate sealant to protect it from water and from products such as body oils or creams which will stain the surface. If you want a painted finish, make sure you choose a water-resistant paint.

THE VARIETY OF GLASS

Glass panels have a great advantage over stud walls: they don't impede the flow of light or make a space feel smaller. In fact, they can add an impression of depth to a room because the eye perceives that a division exists but can still see beyond it. In a bathroom, you should always choose reinforced glass, which comes in a choice of colours ranging from clear to smoky grey, green or blue. One note of caution about this type of glass is that, unless it is pre-coated, you will need to wipe it down regularly with an anti-limescale product to prevent water marks from clouding the surface.

Where greater privacy is needed, for example to screen off a lavatory, consider using opaque, smoked, acid-etched or patterned glass. This will still allow some light through but will give you the privacy you need.

Textured glass is yet another option that goes through cycles of popularity, but the fashionable look now is crazed glass, which has a very dramatic appearance. It looks like a panel of shattered glass but sandwiched between fine protective layers. Random or acid-etched patterning are also contemporary features but are usually custom-made.

Glass bricks – clear or coloured – used to be primarily for industrial use but are now also found in domestic situations. Because of their thickness and texture, they provide a high level of obscurity and sound insulation. They are especially good for constructing functional partitions such as between the lavatory and the rest of the bathroom or for creating a divide between a bedroom and an en-suite facility.

ABOVE By reconfiguring the arrangement of doors to the bathroom, perhaps having two small doors instead of the normal one, you may be able to eke out extra space in a room or better utilise the space you have.

RIGHT Semi-opaque panels or doors provide privacy but also allow a certain amount of light to pass through.

OPPOSITE Sliding doors open back over wall space, unlike hinged doors, which take up space in the room, so, where space is limited, sliding doors provide a useful solution.

LEFT This wet room contains just a shower; it is a space dedicated to one function only so the design scheme and decoration focus on this fact.

RIGHT The half-wall that separates this shower room from the two basins allows the natural light from the roof of the shower room to illuminate both parts of the room.

BELOW This cloakroom only has space for a basin and lavatory. Because the room is small and the facilities are secondary to those of the main bathroom, only a small basin is needed.

SOLO SPACES

Bathrooms don't have to have all their amenities in a single room; you can take some out, or install additional amenities in separate 'solo spaces'. This not only takes pressure off the main bathroom at busy times of day, but also means that you can add new or more up-to-date amenities while still keeping a fully functioning main bathroom.

Another advantage of a solo space is that décor and installation can be specific to the task. For example, a wet room which houses only a shower can be tailored to include a range of nozzles at different heights to give an all-round wash, a bench and a shelf for soaps and lotions. Whereas a shower squeezed into a bathroom might have to make do with a single shower head on a flexible hose, and bottles balanced precariously on the edge of the bath.

And by using the shower over the bath, the whole bathroom will become steamy, fogging up the mirror and making it difficult for the next person to see themself while shaving or brushing their teeth. But in a wet room, there is just one function and that is – take a shower.

Solo spaces can also have a more focused and concentrated feeling because the space is dedicated to a specific function. For example, a whole bathroom decorated in dark blue and green mosaic tiles might be rather overpowering and dark for general day-to-day use, but in a wet room or steam room, the same scheme could be used to make the space feel like a submarine grotto or a deep, cavernous pool.

Steam rooms and saunas are generally contained, if not in their own rooms, then in use-specific cabinets which retain the moisture and/or heat. Because these facilities have a recreational aspect they are generally located separately from the main bathroom, so they are natural 'solo spaces'.

Cloakrooms may also be regarded as solo spaces because they do not include any bathing facilities. Instead they normally comprise an additional

ABOVE You can fit a shower into a small room providing there is space to stand and move around comfortably.

RIGHT A wet room like this can be fitted out as a steam room, although a sealed door is essential to maintain the steam and constant high temperature.

OPPOSITE This pod-like shower stands on a mezzanine above a kitchen. It is designed so that the natural light from the kitchen skylights illuminate it, and also so that the person taking the shower can look out without been seen.

lavatory and hand basin for light daily use. A cloakroom might normally be located on the ground floor or by the main door and is ideal for use as you enter and leave the house or for visitors or tradesmen. As the name suggests, a cloakroom might also provide a place to hang coats.

A similar facility is a useful amenity where there are three or four bedrooms grouped together. The basin and lavatory should ideally be located nearby, along the same hallway or in an adjacent space, or even under the rise of a staircase leading to another floor. These simple basin and lavatory suites can be used to brush teeth and wash hands and faces before going to bed and first thing in the morning.

A solo bath space is rare, but if you have the room there is no reason on earth why a stylish bath can't take centre stage. You are more likely to locate this sort of statement space adjacent to a basin and lavatory, or separated from it by a partition, rather than in a fully enclosed room of its own. Dividing the Space (see pages 18–23) gives some ideas on how to create the feeling of a separate space without there really being one.

OPPOSITE In a hammam or steam room the décor can reflect the relaxed and indulgent atmosphere of the space. Here scale-like, green-glazed tiles have a Moroccan feel, which picks up on the Moorish tradition of going to the hammam.

LEFT This tiny cloakroom has been decorated so that the cupboard doors blend in with the panelling on the lower wall, giving it a neat and unfussy appearance. In a busy cloakroom, where boots are kicked off and grubby hands washed, the panelling also serves to protect the walls.

BED & BATH EN SUITE

Being able to step from bed directly into the shower or bath is an indulgent but efficient way to start the day. And because dressing and undressing accompany bathing, going to bed and rising, by linking these activities, you save time and trouble. But it is better not to include clothes storage in the bathroom. Instead locate wardrobes — if you have the space — in a separate but linked dressing room or, failing that, in the bedroom. If you don't do this, the moisture from the bathroom may damage your clothes.

In a spacious bedroom, it might be possible to carve out space for a separate, walled-off en suite or for the more contemporary version of this — the self-contained shower pod. This comes complete with sealed walls, floor and optional roof and can be placed in a bedroom or even in a deep wardrobe.

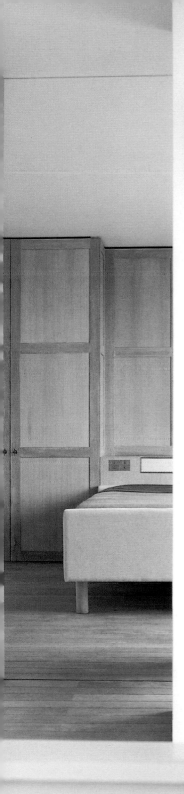
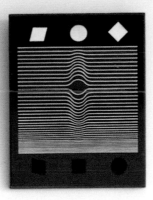

LEFT The thick wood beams of this attic conversion provide a nominal division between the sleeping and washing areas Because of the open-plan aspect of the room, the lavatory has been placed elsewhere in an enclosed and ventilated space. The basin, with its base concealed beneath a curtain, is close by the dressing table. The whole layout of the room is conducive to bathing while having a conversation with a partner or spouse.

THIS PAGE In some properties it may be possible to knock through a wall to gain access to the neighbouring room and create an en-suite bathroom. Most modern homes are designed with at least one en-suite bathroom.

LEFT Designers often link the colours and textures of an en suite to those in the bedroom so that there is a seamless transition from one space to the other.

RIGHT This architectural, enclosed, floor-to-ceiling glass box contains a shower but doesn't impinge on the sense of space or on the décor of the bedroom as the box is almost invisible.

BELOW Good ventilation is essential in bathrooms that open directly onto a bedroom, as here in order to extract steam and odours that might otherwise seep through to the sleeping area.

Some designs are triangular in shape so that they slot neatly into a corner, which is often an area of 'dead' space in a room. You will need efficient ventilation as well as plumbing for the water and drainage, so remember to take this into account in your budget.

Alternatively, if the bedroom is big enough, you might be able to create a shower or bathing area behind the bedhead. By pulling the bed forward into the room and constructing a false wall or partition behind it, you will create a room within a room. The new freestanding wall can conceal a shower and basin or even a bath, but it may not be ideal to install a lavatory in an open-sided space such as this.

RIGHT Waste and water pipes can be disguised or boxed in to create a sense of space. Here the bath has been raised on a ledge that conceals ductwork.

BELOW A number of manufacturers make small baths specifically to fit in awkward and restricted spaces; you can still enjoy the benefit of a warm soak, but may not be able to stretch out flat in the bath.

OPPOSITE This shower is fitted into a triangular space that reflects the architecture. This clever use of an otherwise 'dead' area provides an extra, useful bathing area.

MAKING SPACE

If your bathroom feels cramped, reconfiguring the layout can free up valuable space. For instance, positioning a bath along the wall makes the bath look less dominant and leaves the rest of the space for moving around in. Similarly, lining up the basin, toilet, bath and shower along one wall, gives a clear, uncluttered look.

If you are trying to find space for an extra bathroom, shower room or toilet, it may not be that difficult. First, consider the attic or basement. Head height in an attic is often restricted but there is usually enough room under the apex of the roof to stand full-height in a shower or in front of a basin, and a bath can fit beneath the slope of the roof, as can cupboards or storage units.

RIGHT Although it lies along the lower end of a sloping wall, this bath is still readily accessible from the taller centre area of the room.

BELOW Custom-made units can be designed and fitted to use every available bit of space, so providing the maximum amount of storage.

OPPOSITE A bath can be accommodated under the slope of an attic roof. By placing the tap end at the lowest point and the head end in the centre of the room, you will be able to sit up in and enter and exit the bath easily.

You could use a cellar but may need to tank the walls and floor with a damp-proof membrane. You will also need clever lighting and an efficient air-extraction system. A utility or laundry room might also accommodate a shower enclosure and basin.

The space needed for a lavatory isn't great. A depth of around 120cm (48in) is sufficient, which you might find under the stairs or in a deep hall cupboard.

If it's difficult to locate a lavatory so the waste discharges into the soil stack, consider a macerating toilet system. This takes up about the same space as a conventional toilet but it grinds the waste up so it can flow through a very narrow plastic or copper pipe to the soil stack or to a septic tank.

And finally, another space-saving alternative – if your household is predominantly male – is a wall-mounted urinal.

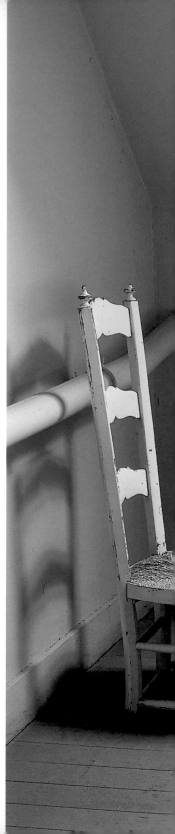

Using outdoor space

- Avoid cosmetic gels and soaps; instead use natural products that won't do damage to the plants.

- A hedge, moveable screen or curtain can be used to provide privacy.

- Adequate drainage avoids a build-up of stagnant water.

- Outdoor bathing at dusk is not advised as mosquitoes are about.

Long hot summers, outdoor sports and the increased use of hot tubs and swimming pools, mean that the garden shower is becoming ever more popular. It can be used to wash away sweat after a game of tennis, to rinse off chlorinated pool water or simply to cool down on a hot day, without having to go indoors.

Outdoor showers can also be used for daily washing during warm weather. Installed in a private, enclosed space on a base of smooth pebbles next to French windows leading from a bedroom to the garden, they offer a fresh, natural start to a summer's day. Showers used in conjunction with a bathing area or hot tub need not be so secluded because the user will normally be wearing a bathing costume.

LEFT This penthouse hot tub is an ideal place to relax and enjoy the view.

ABOVE A metal canopy supports a shower and the floor of smooth pebbles are ideal for bare feet.

RIGHT A simple but dramatic poolside shower.

LEFT A sunken bath beneath folding windows gives a real feeling of bathing outdoors. Setting the bath below the level of the window resolves the problem of privacy.

RIGHT Direct sunlight can be dazzling so on a clear day these blinds can be closed to lessen its impact – and provide privacy – and when light levels are low, the blinds can be raised to make the most of whatever light is available.

ROOMS WITH A VIEW

Bathrooms located on the upper floor of a house or on the loftier levels of an apartment block may be lucky enough to benefit from the view over a leafy park, a skyline of imposing tower blocks or a broad band of sky, so it would be a pity not to enjoy it. There is something magical about watching the weather and the changing seasons while you are relaxing, submerged in water.

Placing a bath, hot tub or spa tub beneath the window of the bathroom, especially if the edge of the bath lines up with the bottom of the window frame, is good planning. The bath won't obstruct the natural light or block the view from other parts of the bathroom, but most importantly, you can look out of the window as you bathe.

But you do not need to have the bath directly beneath the window to enjoy the view; it could be at right angles to the window or even positioned in the centre of the wall directly in front of it.

THIS ELEVATED, UNINTERRUPTED,
PANORAMIC VIEW PROVIDES A
CONSTANTLY CHANGING PLEASURE
TO BE INDULGED IN WHILE RELAXING
IN A WARM, DEEP BATH

THIS PAGE Because this
bath is not overlooked
there is no need to screen
the windows; they can be
left uncovered to frame
the magnificent view.

LEFT This strategically placed panel of opaque glass screens the torso during showering, but the daylight allows the view to be clearly seen.

BELOW A long narrow window high on the wall offers the pleasure of looking out onto the leafy tree tops at bath time.

BELOW RIGHT The mirror above the basin reflects the light and view from the window behind, so that the person using the basin can enjoy it while washing.

Some bathrooms have a skylight in the ceiling. Instead of just thinking of this as a means of bringing light into the room, consider it as a design feature and position your bath or tub right underneath it so that you can lie back and watch the clouds scudding by.

MAINTAIN YOUR MODESTY

Being able to look out can be pleasurable, but having people looking in is bad, so modesty must be taken into consideration if you are bathing directly in front of a window which is overlooked. You may need have a half-curtain to screen the lower part of the window, or a blind that pulls up from the bottom and fixes into brackets on the lower half of the window frame. Alternatively, you might install a panel of opaque glass in the lower section of the window or use the technologically advanced Privalite glass that turns from clear to opaque at the press of a button. A light but densely pleated cotton voile curtain is a softer and more feminine solution, and can be easily taken down and washed to keep its appearance pristine.

THIS PAGE This bath is positioned beneath a back-lit panel of semi-opaque glass which gives the impression of being a roof light.

Bringing light to a windowless room

- Use a porthole instead of a square or rectangular frame for an unusual 'fake' window.

- Put semi-opaque glass panels in a door to bring light in from a hallway.

- Mirrors can be angled in order to bounce daylight around corners.

- Use a projector to create a surreal window with a view on a plain white wall.

Many bathrooms in modern apartment blocks are located internally, without windows, while in older houses, an additional bathroom may be installed in an attic or basement, again without any natural light. In an attic bathroom, you could install a regular skylight or a tubular one with a silvered internal surface, which funnels and magnifies the light from outside. In a basement it may be possible to replace part of the paving directly above and adjacent to the basement with glass bricks.

Where it isn't possible to create any sort of window, you can devise the illusion of one by using a panel of opaque glass in the wall or ceiling and fitting daylight bulbs behind. The clear blue-white light will fill the room, and give the space a more open and inviting appearance.

ABOVE An impression of daylight can be brought into a windowless space through the use of artificial light and mirrored panels to double the effect.

RIGHT A deep well skylight floods an attic bathroom with natural light.

PRACTICALITIES

Having decided what you want, the next step is to evaluate what is feasible and practicable in terms of cost. As a general guideline, you need to allocate fifty per cent of your budget for materials, fixtures and fittings, and fifty per cent for labour. Moving and installing pipes, electrics and waste outlets can be expensive so remember to allow for this. If you are increasing your use of water by adding a bathroom, you also need to check that your boiler and water tank can cope with the extra demand.

Especially if you are on a tight budget, you should spend some time shopping around for your fixtures and fittings. Sometimes it can be more economical to mix and match rather than buy a complete bathroom suite. If you buy a simple lavatory and hand basin, for instance, you may have more to spend on an eye-catching designer bath or steam cabin.

ABOVE An inexpensive bath can be given a more glamorous appearance by the use of interesting designer taps.

RIGHT Bathrooms that are en suite to a bedroom should be compatible in style with the overall scheme. It is better to choose simple shapes rather than overly ornate or decorative ones.

OPPOSITE Feature lighting, concealed under shelves and in the shower, need to be installed by a professional.

LEFT Old baths can be restored and recycled, but make sure that they can be connected to modern plumbing. Opting for a floor-standing tap and shower unit can skirt round any difficulties.

RIGHT Bulk-buying a single type of stone or ceramic tile for the floors, walls and ceiling, may help to reduce costs as well as providing a unified look.

BELOW Cladding the side of a bath with bath panels will provide a certain amount of insulation which can help to keep the bath water warmer for longer.

When it comes to building and fitting, always employ recommended professionals who belong to a recognised trade association. For a radical makeover or new-build you may also need an architect or structural engineer.

ENVIRONMENTAL ISSUES

Finding ways of economising on your water and energy use in your bathroom is not only good for the environment but might save you money, too. Bathroom manufacturers have been quick to respond to environmental concerns, introducing dual-flush cisterns for lavatories (see page 111), basins with a shallow section for shaving or brushing your teeth, and cartridges in the tap or shower that warn when you are exceeding half-flow.

Fixing dripping taps, using a plug in the wash basin, turning the tap off while brushing your teeth and taking a shower rather than a bath are simple cost-cutting, eco-friendly measures you can easily take.

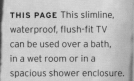

THIS PAGE This slimline, waterproof, flush-fit TV can be used over a bath, in a wet room or in a spacious shower enclosure.

Adding sound and vision

- Electrical equipment in a bathroom must be specially designed to be moisture-sealed and steam- and water-safe.

- Always have TVs and speakers installed by an approved fitter.

- Sit in the bath to gauge the height for fitting the TV screen and if you want to see it from the shower as well, make sure you can.

If you want a hedonistic bathing experience, forget the old battery-operated radio balanced precariously on the rim of the bath or the magazine getting soggy in the damp atmosphere of the bathroom. Now you can install speakers and television screens in your bathroom and enjoy your favourite music, films or TV programmes while you soak.

Sealed speakers connected to a radio or CD player elsewhere in the home can be recessed in the walls or ceiling and controlled in the bathroom via a finger-touch panel. Slimline waterproof TV screens fit into any wall which can then be tiled or plastered to ensure a perfectly sealed fit. The screen is heated to prevent it misting up – it looks like a mirror when the TV is off – and there's even a floating remote control.

ABOVE Small round waterproof speakers have been fitted onto the wall beneath the shower.

RIGHT The image on this TV screen set at higher than eye-level almost looks like a painting on the wall.

Quality is key in this spacious minimal bathroom which boasts a generous washbasin, discreet shower cubicle and stone-clad walls. The wooden bench brings a sense of comfort and the mirror covering the whole of one wall underlines the feeling of luxury.

Inspirational Styles

Lifestyle and fashion trends are increasingly influencing design in the home but when it comes to bathrooms, their effect is usually more subtle and gradual. In addition, most bathroom design is constrained by the practicalities of the room – the need for safety, durability and water- and heat-resistance – but with developments in materials and technology, a growing range of options is now available.

TOP LEFT This monotone scheme is simple but stylish. The mirror frames the back wall but also provides protection from the spray of the shower, as will the curtain that falls to the right of the bath, yet none of these devices are immediately obvious.

TOP RIGHT A mix of classic and contemporary – a restored silver-sided roll-top bath is set against crisp white walls and black-painted woodwork, so that the bath is the centre of attention. The black recessed shelves keep towels close at hand and ready for use.

BOTTOM LEFT This ethnic-inspired design uses unusual conical bases to support the basins and a handmade wooden ladder as a towel rail. Both are in keeping with the raw plaster-effect walls and timber supports of the ceiling.

BOTTOM RIGHT Empire style for the twenty-first century – this scheme incorporates furniture, fittings and flooring from several different eras, but by keeping the palette to simple black-and-white, the diverse elements are cleverly brought together.

Developments that are having an effect on the way our bathrooms function and look include: refinements in photographic printing techniques, which have brought colour and pattern to ceramics and laminate finishes; new fabrication and strengthening techniques for glass, which result in the material being used to create walls, baths and basins, thus adding a sculptural element to contemporary wash spaces; and the further evolution of man-made materials such as Corian and PVC, which give more flexibility in casting, enabling the creation of shapes that are tailor-made to fit and that can have unusual profiles if required.

Your choice of bathroom style is a very personal matter and, once again, there are many options. Choose from sleekly minimal bathrooms, bathrooms that embrace the return of colour, new sensually curvy bathrooms, comforting spa-style bathrooms or idiosyncratic 'me' style bathrooms where you can really let your decorative imagination have free rein.

MINIMAL

For the ultimate in minimal design, many interior designers have taken their inspiration from commercial spaces, especially modern five-star hotels. In these busy, much-used environments, the policy is to surround the guests with a feeling of comfort and luxury, yet for the bathing spaces to be efficient and functional. In such schemes the floor plan and layout are a priority; the space allocated for hotel en-suite bathrooms is usually restricted but it should not feel so. The guest must be able to use and move around the space with ease and without a sense of confinement.

The materials used in these bathrooms are hard-wearing but attractive, and convey a sense of richness and quality. Marble, mica-flecked polished granite and satin-smooth sandstone are popular but black or white resins are also used, as well as glass.

The saying 'less is more" encapsulates the minimal style – but where fewer elements meet the eye, they have to be of the highest possible calibre;

RIGHT To ensure that minimal does not mean cold, clinical and uncomfortable, these white, unencumbered spaces need subtle and well-sited lighting.

OPPOSITE To avoid the harsh effect of bright daylight a calico blind is used as a diffuser, creating a soft glow and a muted ambience in the room.

IN MINIMAL BATHROOMS QUALITY IS A PRIORITY. THERE IS NOTHING TO DISTRACT THE EYE — THE CLEAN LINES AND UNCLUTTERED APPEARANCE FOCUS ATTENTION ON THE FINISHES AND FURNITURE

THIS PAGE In a minimal bathroom storage is important because the surface must be kept clear, except for a few carefully selected items.

LEFT Where the colour palette is limited and the shapes are regular and linear, the eye is drawn to texture. Here, the mottled appearance of the concrete bath becomes the dominant feature of the room.

RIGHT The smooth curved shape of the bath is framed and highlighted by the black panel against which it is set. Even the stepped detailing on the walls becomes an architectural accent.

BELOW Here angular shapes play one against another to emphasise the graphic qualities of the basin and mirror.

the elements of the minimal bathroom are not disguised among a plethora of colours, fixtures or embellishments.

Against the plain and simple layout of a minimal bathroom, the accessories and fittings become the focus – like a stunning bag or great piece of jewellery against a simple shift dress. Instead of there being a traditional tap, water might run into the bath via a cascade from a shelf, or a beautifully sculpted radiator might take centre stage rather than there being a rather ordinary one that is banished to the sidelines.

The minimal bathroom also requires wall-hung sanitaryware rather than toilets and bidets on pedestals or basins set into cabinets, as these give a feeling of bulk and restrict the flow of light. And finally, minimal bathrooms demand ample storage space so surfaces remain pristine and clutter-free.

COLOUR SPLASH

Colour is making a notable return to the bathroom. The latest trend is for a single, vibrantly coloured 'signature' piece to establish a scheme or break up the sometimes clinical appearance of an all-white bathroom.

The 'signature' piece is usually a bath or basin and can be in any of a wide range of colours from brilliant orange or lime green to raspberry pink, rather than pale pastel or 'a hint of...'. These single, colourful items become the room's focus; they make a scheme individual and memorable, but because the colour is bold the shape of the piece is usually simple, with a streamlined profile and the taps and accessories that accompany it are understated.

Few schemes use more than one 'signature' piece because, especially in today's compact bathrooms, too much colour can be overwhelming and may

TOP A single, brightly coloured basin can update a plain white bathroom.

ABOVE This 'signature' bath is in a vivid resin which will not fade or stain.

RIGHT This bath and basin surround are in a synthetic material which has a solid, stone-like quality but is warm to the touch.

OPPOSITE Colourful and 'busy' digitally printed tiles contrast with the simplicity of the white basin in front.

LEFT Here, wall paint has been colour-matched to the exact shade of dusky pink used on the inner faces of this unusual suite. Custom-matching paint service is widely available.

RIGHT Co-ordinate the outside of a roll-top bath to suit any scheme – just ensure that you use heat-resistant paint suitable for a metal surface.

BELOW In a tiny cloakroom a small, colourful wash basin need be the only element of colour. Its presence is enough to make a statement and help define the space.

make the space feel smaller and cramped. Even in a large bathroom, the impact of a vivid red bath or dramatic green basin would be diminished if it were mixed with other pieces of the same or different colour.

If you are keeping a good-quality white bathroom suite but you still want to add colour, you can do so elsewhere in the décor. Coloured paint on doors, walls or ceilings is the simplest option. Another is coloured tiles. Colourful mosaic tiles can be used to cover areas exposed to water, such as around the bath, behind the basin or inside the shower, or there are larger ceramic tiles, colourfully printed with graphic designs, that can be mixed and matched. Photographic transfer tiles and laminate finishes are the latest in the world of tile design. These put not only colour and pattern firmly on the agenda, but also texture. Some companies create tiles using your own photographic images, so that you can achieve a truly personal and customised look.

Another place to add colour to a traditional white bathroom is the bath panel or built-in units and cupboards. These can be updated or transformed with paint or a bright laminate. Although matt paint finishes are fashionable, you can create a light-reflecting lacquer effect with a layer of high-gloss paint.

NEW WAVE

The sensuous curve or wave is big news in bathroom design; it is found not only in shower enclosures, basin and baths, but also as part of the architecture of the room in the form of full- or half-height room dividers. It offers a soft, caressing, fluid shape which fits comfortably in a room where the body is usually naked and vulnerable. The curve is also visually more restful and relaxing to look at than a hard, sharp right angle.

Curvy basins, baths and even room dividers can be created in easily mouldable, man-made materials such as Corian and resin composites. These are tactile, soft and warm to the touch, which is in keeping with the sensual and comforting quality of the curving shapes. The wrap-around qualities of interlocking curves and spirals also make these the perfect shapes in which to set a shower – all the water is contained within so there is no need for a door or screen. And on a practical note, since curves have no joins, they are easy to wipe clean and won't suffer from leaking corners or splitting joints.

BELOW LEFT A conceptual ebb-and-flow design encompasses all the main features here – basin, bath, lavatory and shelf.

THIS PAGE This bath is shaped like an ample female figure. The shapely curves are echoed in the ammonite-like shower enclosure in opaque acrylic, which helps to obscure the view of the bath from the window.

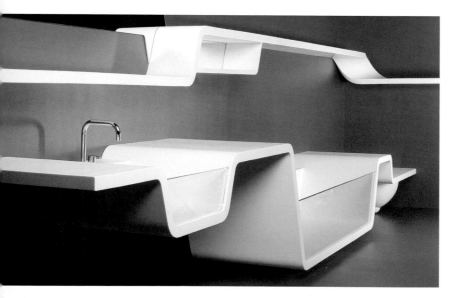

THIS PAGE Although a shower is enclosed within this curved wall, its outer face makes a pleasing architectural contribution to the space around it. The corridor area is illuminated by low-level lights, which at night will wash up the walls and exaggerate the lines of this interesting feature.

OPPOSITE ABOVE As much a work of art as a bath, this curved reclining surface encased in a glass box is a spectacular piece of engineering and design, yet it looks so simple. The simplicity also adds to the feeling of calmness and tranquillity that seems to emanate from the design.

OPPOSITE BELOW Waves and curves are extremely aesthetically pleasing and are smooth on the eye as well as to the touch. This undulating, glass-fronted surface provides a really neat shallow basin that combines form and function to perfection.

A number of contemporary bath and basin designs incorporate the wave or curve as a sculptural feature encased within transparent glass panels. Here, it is the beauty and fluidity of the line that is the primary feature – the glass shows it off to perfection – with the functionality of the piece a secondary benefit. These spectacular designs are usually set in a prominent position and may be the focal point of a minimal bathroom scheme (see above).

As well as man-made Corian and resin composites that are easily poured and formed into continuous rounded shapes for baths and basins, metals such as stainless steel and even wood can be made into attractive curvilinear shapes. In the case of wood, panels or planks can be faceted together in sections and, using techniques originally employed in the making of clinker-built ship hulls, the wood can be formed into a curve and used for architectural partitions or bath surrounds.

LEFT In calm, nature-inspired surroundings, it is important to keep the hardware simple. This combination spout and tap is streamlined and functional; by plumbing it in the wall, the rim of the bath remains uncluttered.

RIGHT This sybaritic spa-style bathroom, with its sunken bath and dark wood accessories has a strong modern Asian feel. As in oriental philosophy, Yin and Yang, or dark and light, are in perfect balance.

SPA STYLE

The term 'spa' originally referred to the sites of curative mineral springs where the water was used for bathing and drinking in an effort to heal and detoxify the body. Nowadays, spa culture is still founded on these ideals but has expanded to include ways of releasing stress, with the focus on both physical and mental wellbeing.

To bring the holistic feeling of a spa to a domestic bathroom, you need a design that gives a sense of peace and calm. Neutral colours help achieve this; these shades have an affinity which gives them an easy harmony so you will rarely go wrong with beiges, browns, greys and greens. And also use natural materials such as wood, bamboo and stone to create another link with nature and the outdoors. For inspiration, look to the East where meditation, contemplation and simplicity go hand in hand with oriental religions.

The sunken bath is often a feature of a spa-style bathroom. Generally oversized, it feels like a natural pool, allowing the bather to float and relax completely without the restrictions of a conventional bath.

Moving water has also been proven to aid relaxation. Firstly, the sound is said to be calming, so a feature or sculpture with flowing or trickling water is often incorporated into a spa-style bathroom. Then there is the sense of wellbeing that moving water in the bath itself brings to the body. In a spa bathroom, whirlpool and Jacuzzi appliances often provide that. The jets, aerated bubbles and pulse features create eddies of water that gently massage the body, helping muscles to relax and so relieve tension. And there are also those who claim that the feeling of warm weightlessness and the constant low-level massage in a thermostatically controlled environment can benefit sprains, rheumatism, cramps, sciatica and lumbago.

ABOVE Organic materials such as wood evoke a feeling of contact with nature and where, as in the case of this rustic-style bathroom, the wood has been left completely unfinished, there is a strong sense of the outside having come indoors.

LEFT The bath or tub is often the centrepiece of a spa room. It is designed for indulgent relaxation and calm contemplation as well as for deep cleansing.

OPPOSITE Sliding doors or large windows opening out onto a deck, balcony or garden increase the visual and sensual enjoyment of the room as well as giving a feeling of close contact with nature, the seasons and the environment.

'ME' SPACE

Because a bathroom, especially one that is en suite to your bedroom, is primarily a private space, it is somewhere you can let your decorative imagination have free rein. In the rest of the home, especially in common and shared spaces where visitors and guests are entertained, it is usual for the décor to be restrained rather than overpowering, but in your own, intimate space, you can indulge yourself.

Whether you yearn for an exotic Moorish temple, the Neptune-like splendour of a subterranean pebble-filled grotto, or for a gallery to display your favourite prints, photographs or collection of tropical fish, the 'me' space bathroom can provide it. This type of bathroom is all about escapism; it is a way of transporting yourself to another part of your mind, to a place where you can immerse yourself in your own fantasies.

ABOVE Sometimes a bath will be the starting point for a decorative theme; this period-style double-ended bath has overtones of the Empire period that are picked up in the silhouette painting and pastoral wallpaper panels.

RIGHT This simple but social space is somewhere to talk to a friend or soak alone if you close the door on the hustle and bustle of the world outside.

OPPOSITE Having your favourite things around makes a bathroom special.

But when you are decorating a 'me' space, you still need to keep in mind the practical aspects of the bathroom. Baths and showers bring with them damp and moisture which can damage paintings and prints unless they are sealed and well-framed. Delicate or antique fabrics may fade and rot. You also need to avoid sharp edges and fragile glass or mirrored accessories that might crack or break into dangerous shards.

If lavish decoration isn't your thing, then creating your 'me' space bathroom may simply be about having time to yourself, away from the hubbub of the household. Your 'me' space bathroom can then be the place where you listen, uninterrupted, to your favourite radio programme, watch the next instalment of a TV soap, or unwind to a favourite piece of music while you soak in deep, warm water (see pages 52–53 for how to add sound and vision to your bathroom experience).

Using chromotherapy

- Link scented candles and bath oils to the colour themes – lavender with blue, vetiver with green, and so on.

- A single circuit of lights with gels or tinted bulbs is fine, but cutting-edge schemes feature fibre-optic and LED illumination.

- If coloured lighting doesn't appeal, try coloured accessories such as towels and candles.

Chromotherapy, a form of colour healing based on Ayurvedic principles, is said to have a holistic effect on mind and body. Ayurveda asserts that red promotes good circulation, energy and stimulation, whereas blue is calm and meditative and green is said to balance mind and body and promote renewal and growth.

Using any one of these colours in a wash of light across a plain white bathroom, or installing one of the latest illuminated baths or basins can have a dramatic effect not only visually, but may also make you feel better and enhance the enjoyment of your bath. For fun and enjoyment you could also create you own blends of colours, mixing red and blue hues for a violet tone or red and yellow for a hot orange.

ABOVE Illuminated tubs and basins are made from polyethylene and have a water-sealed light inside.

RIGHT Even a shower can be made to change colour.

OPPOSITE Some coloured-light baths come with a remote control so that you can change the colour as you bathe.

A modern take on the roll-top bath takes pride of place in a bathroom where all the elements have been carefully chosen to create a traditional look with a contemporary twist.

Sourcebook

A well designed room isn't just about the allocation of space and the use of light; it is the sum of all the individual pieces, the bringing together of individual accessories and items of furniture to make a complete and co-ordinated scheme.

In a bathroom the primary task is to combine function and aesthetics, blending hardware, such as taps and radiators, and furniture – in this case basins and bidets, baths and showers – with flooring and wall coverings so that the space is clean and efficient yet comfortable and interesting to be in.

To achieve the right mix it is essential to look at each aspect of the bathroom in turn and to 'marry' shapes and styles as well as introducing contrast and texture. Although the all-white bathroom with chrome fittings can appear bland or clinical, with some unusual choices it can be interesting. For example, a large oval centrally located white bath will be an eye-catching feature, a swan-neck floor-mounted mixer tap will accentuate the curves of the bath and a mosaic floor will contrast with the smooth, sleek lines of bath and tap.

Similarly, in a small cloakroom, pale colours make the most of the available light and space, but a vivid blue glass hand basin and a 'coiled-spring' radiator ensure the room is interesting and memorable.

TOP LEFT Fine-spray shower nozzles are one of a number of recent designs that pick up on the rain-shower effect. They give a soft mist-like sprinkle of water rather than a regular spray.

TOP RIGHT Radiators in bathrooms are usually sculptural or decorative and are often used as towel rails now that underfloor heating is the most popular way to warm this room of the house.

BOTTOM LEFT This magnifying mirror is an integral part of a basin design by Jaime Hayon who combines elements of tables and chairs with baths and basins.

BOTTOM RIGHT This spring or coil radiator is long and slim and takes up a minimal amount of wall space, but because of the large surface area provided by the coils, it emits a substantial amount of heat.

WALLS & FLOORS

Because of the nature of bathrooms, walls and floors have to be hard-wearing and resilient yet comfortable against bare skin, and they also must be capable of coping with splashes and puddles of water yet be quick and simple to wipe clean.

For years, glazed ceramic tiles fulfilled all these requirements and because they came in a rainbow assortment of colours, they suited innumerable bathroom schemes. Now, though, designers have been turning their attention to nature and have started to use stone and wood on floors and walls instead of or in addition to ceramics. At the same time, manufacturers have developed cutting-edge ranges of man-made materials for this purpose – for example, vinyl, rubber and resin, glass and concrete.

ABOVE The simple one-colour/one-material scheme for the walls and floors makes the bath an eye-catching feature.

RIGHT The hard blackness of the roughly hewn slate panels covering the bath is softened by the rich red, finely grained wood on the walls and floor.

OPPOSITE The contrast between the mosaic on the floor and the decoratively grained stone of the wall and bath plinth gives character to this otherwise minimal bathroom.

Now the possibilities for different looks and effects are endless but the priorities remain the same. Whatever you are using to cover either a bathroom wall or floor, it is essential to ensure that there are no gaps for water to seep through and damage the structural elements beneath. The slow drip or seepage of water can do irreparable long-term harm to the fabric of a building, especially in older houses with wooden joists, so always check that the flooring around the edge of the bath and the walls inside a shower enclosure are well-fitting and tightly sealed.

Although the stone and concrete finishes found in bathrooms today usually consist of just a thin veneer or facing of the material, you still need to keep in mind the weight they will bring to bear, especially if you have old floorboards and beams. It could be that you will require additional support in the form of strengthened joists or

ABOVE Many people prefer smooth bathroom surfaces like polished stone or sealed wood as they are easy to clean.

LEFT Natural stone comes in a wide range of colours and variations; even within the slate family you can see green, red and ochre hues. These can be used to make a rich, patchwork-like pattern of floor and wall tiles.

OPPOSITE Rough-hewn stone gives a feeling of strength and history to this cloakroom; its natural texture makes a superb contrast to the smooth, man-made concrete floor.

walls. You may also find that it is necessary to underlay the stone with sheets of plywood. This creates a level and stable base, which will help protect the stone from bending and cracking. Whatever you choose, always use a professional installer.

Bathrooms are also prime locations for underfloor heating, especially if you are using hard, cold flooring such as stone and concrete. Heating elements encased in a protective shell can be laid under the whole floor so that the chill is removed and the surface is pleasant to walk on with bare feet. Another advantage of underfloor heating is that the heat rises and permeates the whole room, thus doing away with the need for wall-hung radiators – although a heated towel rail is a useful addition.

When you are choosing tiles or pavers of stone, ceramic or even cork, you need to balance the size of the tile with the scale of the room. For example, in a spacious bathroom, you can afford to select large tiles but in a smaller space, such as a shower or wet room, smaller units look in better proportion.

The care and maintenance of bathroom walls and floors is important, firstly for hygienic reasons but secondly because of the effects of steam and water. Wood used in a bathroom should be specially treated and sealants and coatings on stone and granite may need to be renewed from time to time.

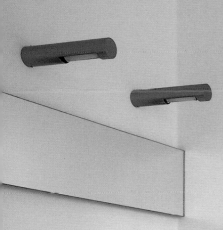

OPPOSITE TOP LEFT With the walls and basin stand clad in simple stone squares, the intricate mosaic floor becomes the focus of attention.

OPPOSITE TOP RIGHT Bold patterns work in a spacious bathroom; here striped wallpaper and a frieze are complemented by a starburst on the floor.

OPPOSITE BELOW If you go for a complex pattern on the walls, balance it with a plain floor covering.

THIS PAGE The walls of this shower room are clad in Corian, a blend of natural and acrylic components. Impermeable, it can be joined to create a seamless appearance.

BATHS

Until relatively recently, bath-tub designs were limited so frustrated architects started to create their own designs using today's cutting-edge materials. Philippe Starck and Antonio Citterio are among those who have taken bath design into the twenty-first century.

Taking the lead from the East, where the shower is regarded as a means of washing and cleansing and the bath or tub is a place for a long soak or a sociable place to relax with friends, the bath has taken on a more glamorous and decorative role. It is often now the focal point of a room of its own.

Orient-inspired soaking baths are shorter, much deeper and often wider than the average European bath and, as a result, the water stays warmer for longer. They usually also have a step inside that doubles as a seat.

Then there are other types of bath that benefit from a range of technical advances. You can now have water jets and massage pumps (see pages 72–75)

ABOVE Wall-mounted taps and hose leave the bath with an uninterrupted, handsome profile.

LEFT This wooden bath takes inspiration from Japanese soaking tubs. The wood must be properly prepared and maintained to stop it from drying out and cracking.

RIGHT Concrete poured on-site allows a bath to be made specifically to fit a size or shape that might not accommodate a factory-produced design.

THIS PAGE Modern production techniques allow bath and base to be formed in a single mould. They look solid but are often surprisingly light.

OPPOSITE TOP LEFT Designer Jaime Hayon uses the delicate legs usually seen on a table or chair to give this bath the appearance of an elegant piece of furniture.

OPPOSITE TOP RIGHT Steps alongside a recessed round tub offer a place to sit and relax.

or lighting (see pages 80–81). You can even have an 'infinity' bath – one with an overflow rim so the water gently overlaps, drains out and recirculates.

A RANGE OF MATERIALS

Most baths are made of synthetic materials, the main ones being acrylic, which is warm and light, and resin, which is stronger than acrylic and feels more solid. These materials offer more scope for creating interesting shapes than the materials of the past. They are also lighter, making it possible to have a large round bath or deep oval tub without risking structural problems.

But there are many other possiblities. The Eastern influence has brought with it wooden tubs and these sit well in spa-style bathrooms (see pages 72–75). Glass, stone and concrete are also popular. There are all-glass baths (see page 71) or those where the glass is used as a single panel along the facing edge of a concrete or stone bath. The shape of stone baths is governed by the rigidity of the material; they tend to be square or rectangular.

Concrete is a versatile material for a bath as it can be poured into a mould or wood-shuttered shape on site. This allows a bath to be created to fit a space exactly: if you have a long, narrow, boxy or awkward irregular shape where a conventional manufactured bath won't fit, you can easily have one made to your exact specifications.

ABOVE In an infinity bath, the water flows over the rim to be recycled from an outer reservoir.

The ever-popular roll-top bath

- ■ 'Slipper' roll-tops are higher at one end; 'Plunger' roll-tops are named after their plunge waste outlet; the 'Bateau' is an extra-deep, French, boat-style double-ender bath.

- ■ Styles of foot are 'Spoon', 'Claw' and 'Ball and Lion'.

- ■ Use a 50:50 mix of vinegar and water to remove any build-up of limescale from old vitreous enamel.

Originally made in cast iron with an interior of fired enamel, the classic roll-top bath, with its distinctive curved rim and ornate claw feet, was solid, weighty, inherently cold and prone to chip. The roll-top style continues to thrive, but is now made in ceramic, acrylic, resin and even copper. Its graceful lines have made it a timeless masterpiece that still works well with modern fittings and in contemporary locations.

With the continuing popularity of the original roll-top baths, which were produced between the 1880s and the 1930s, there are many specialist companies who repair and restore on-site. They offer re-enamelling services, in a range of colours as well as white, and they can sometimes provide details of the bath's history and previous residences.

OPPOSITE Copper baths are usually coated with a protective lacquer which will come off if you use polish. They only require an occasional wash with tepid soapy water.

LEFT Framed by an oval shower curtain that mimics the bath's shape, this roll-top looks elegant and graceful.

BELOW LEFT The aged, distressed appearance of a reclaimed roll-top bath complements the exposed brick wall.

RIGHT The classic roll-top bath suits any surroundings, from period to contemporary.

ABOVE Ceiling mounted, rain-shower panels produce a wide, fine spray.

ABOVE RIGHT A combination of a large fixed shower rose and a hand-held nozzle allows for thorough cleansing.

OPPOSITE A bank of six wall-mounted jets and an overhead rose give a powerful flow of water. Splashes are contained by the large, clear glass enclosure with its centrally located drain.

SHOWERS

Showers are a quick and easy way of having a thorough wash, they use a fraction of the energy and water of a bath, and the temperature of the water can be thermostatically controlled.

But now showers have ancillary amenities. There are showers with steam and aromatherapy facilities; wet rooms that are, in effect, one big shower enclosure; showers that deliver water like falling rain or that spray it from all sides as well as from above; and showers with built-in seats — ideal for people who might find it difficult to 'climb' over the edge of a bath.

With the rise in popularity of the shower, the styling and design of the shower enclosure have advanced hand in hand with the efficiency of the delivery of the water. One contemporary trend is for power showers. These use an additional pump or high-pressure water booster to deliver the water with a more intense force, but power showers can use up to fifty per cent more water than a standard shower.

Another trend is for more than one shower jet.
Additional jets can be plumbed into walls or panels so
the body is sprayed with water from all angles.

The fashion in shower-enclosure design is for near-
invisibility or for the enclosure to be treated as a
sculptural feature. The near-invisible shower enclosure
features frameless shower-screen panels attached to the
wall or, by using discreet metal brackets, configured
into a freestanding, walk-in module . New self-cleaning
and 'non-stick' glass ensure that these box-like
structures retain their transparency.

Although declining in popularity, shower curtains
can still be found, though mainly in conjunction with
an over-bath shower. Curtains hang from a pole along
the single open side of the bath or on a circular, hooped
frame around a projecting shower. In a plainly
decorated bathroom a colourful shower curtain can

ABOVE A circular shower
curtain over a deep,
custom-made bath makes
the one space dual-
purpose. The plain white
curtain is in keeping with
the simple style and décor.

LEFT The end of a corridor
or passageway could be
annexed and waterproofed
to provide a simple shower.

OPPOSITE This wet room
is minimal but practical.
The generous space allows
for unhindered washing
and the bench can be used
as a shelf as well as
somewhere to sit down
and relax afterwards.

brighten the scheme and in certain settings a plain plastic shower curtain may be used as a waterproof liner for an outer curtain of fabric.

WATERPROOFING AND VENTILATION

Walk-in showers and wet rooms are designed to be totally waterproof; to achieve this, the walls and floors are tanked or lined with a waterproof membrane before the wall and floor coverings are applied. Drainage is usually via a drain in the centre of a gently sloping floor.

Ventilation is another important practical aspect that you should take into consideration. Good ventilation is essential because steam builds up quickly and can temporarily decrease visibility in the bathroom. And in the long term, steam and the moisture it produces can cause mould. If your shower enclosure is tiled, used a mould-inhibiting grout and check regularly that the grout is in good condition.

ABOVE LEFT This chimney-like structure contains a walk-in shower with a deep step to prevent water from flowing out onto the bathroom floor.

LEFT A graceful Moorish archway opens onto a sunken shower and bath tub with steps that double as a seat. A small skylight above the shower allows daylight in.

RIGHT The perfect solution for a large and busy family household – a row of showers that can be used simultaneously.

ABOVE This ammonite-shaped, walk-in shower enclosure looks unusual and attractive and also offers the user a generous space in which to wash.

LEFT This simple all-in-one shower could be installed indoors or out.

BELOW This shower enclosure with seat is also a steam cabinet in which you can use aromatherapy oils to scent the water vapour. Some brands of enclosure also have variable and coloured-lighting options.

LEFT The elliptical lines of this hand-held shower are echoed in the shape of the on/off handle.

LEFT CENTRE The most common form of shower head is known as a rose; this one is wall-mounted.

LEFT BELOW Fine jets of water emerge from the metal disc in this colourful, telephone-like shower head. Clean and de-scale regularly to prevent the build up of limescale which will reduce its effectiveness.

RIGHT This 'rake' style shower head, shown turned off and in use, has a series of perforated bars which release the water in a dense, focused spray.

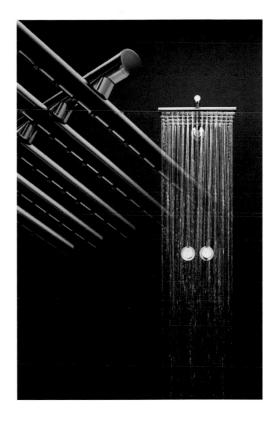

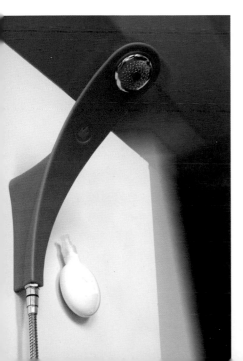

SHOWER HEADS

Shower heads come in many shapes and sizes and offer a variety of flow strengths and effects. They can be fixed – generally overhead – or they may be height-adjustable, fixed to a hose that slides up and down on a pole or detachable from the pole so that they can also be hand-held.

The flow of water is governed by the rose or nozzle and in many cases nowadays these are adjustable, providing a range of effects from a needle-like direct jet to a soft, sensual stream or the massaging quality of a pulsating flow.

Current trends also include multi-nozzle showers with a number of wall-mounted heads at different heights and angles, and the 'rain shower', which disperses the water across a plate and through hundreds of tiny holes to give the bather the sense of standing outside in the rain.

Maintenance of shower heads is important, especially if you live in a hard-water area. You should clean your shower heads regularly to prevent the build-up of limescale which will diminish their power and efficiency.

LEFT In a cloakroom where there is usually just a basin and lavatory, designers often look for an unusual or interesting bowl to make a statement. Here, a hand-hewn, trough-like concrete basin has been set into a surround of rich, dark wood. The finishing touch is the single-spout lever tap.

BASINS, BIDETS, ETC

Matching bathroom suites consisting of a hand basin, bath and toilet are still the norm, but hand basins do not have to be part of a matching suite. A dramatic stand-alone basin may be made from an infinite number of materials such as slate, granite or a rough-hewn block of stone. It can be of up-to-the-minute, fashionable glass or you might use an antique bowl discreetly adapted to accommodate a plughole.

There are many styles of basins, bidets and lavatories and the terminology used to describe their method of installation goes some way to defining their appearance. The most traditional are pedestal-mounted – on a column or other base fixed to the floor. Most classic and period-style ranges are this type.

'Cabinet-mounted' is a term generally applied to basins. These can be set flush into a base unit or may be semi-inset, with the front edge protruding.

ABOVE This altar-style structure supports a small steel basin recessed in the top, leaving a broad edge that is useful for towels and toiletries. The compact basin is almost lost in the volume of the poured and polished concrete stand, but together they make a really strong statement.

TOP LEFT Standing on a plinth like a piece of art, this black ceramic basin, inspired by a calabash, is an attention-grabbing piece of bathroom décor.

TOP RIGHT Countersunk beneath a marble surround, this beaten metal basin has an antiqued finish.

CENTRE LEFT Resting on a simple wooden frame that echoes its shape, this rectangular white ceramic basin looks sleek and modern and is the perfect foil to the textured bronze tiles behind.

CENTRE RIGHT This glass bowl looks as though it is balanced on the surface below but it is in fact plumbed and secured via the central waste outlet.

BOTTOM LEFT To keep the clean lines and visual attractiveness of a special basin uncluttered, store creams and lotions in a wall-mounted, mirrored cupboard above.

BOTTOM RIGHT Pipe work is usually concealed in a unit or behind a plinth, but here the pipes have been burnished and exposed to form an integral part of the overall design.

THIS PAGE This glass trough, raised on a plinth that conceals the waste outlet, has a light and airy feel which is ideal for a small bathroom. The basin is displayed as an object of beauty rather than something utilitarian; all hints of its practical purpose, such as the taps and spout, are positioned so they do not interfere with the visual effect.

But most contemporary bathrooms opt for wall-hung suites that are fixed via a frame to the wall so the basin, toilet or bidet is cantilevered out, leaving the floor area clear. This is ideal for a minimal look (see pages 58–63), or for bathrooms or cloakrooms that have limited space.

LAVATORY OPTIONS

Back-to-wall or 'concealed-cistern' lavatories are fitted to the floor and abut a stud wall that conceals the cistern. Only the handle or push-button flush mechanism is on show. The boxing-in of the cistern can double as a storage shelf for toilet rolls and towels. If you have this type of installation, ensure there is access to the cistern in case there are any problems. Close-coupled or

LEFT Artisan-style, hand-crafted units provide a support for a basin and two side units that can double as stools or shelves for clothes or towels.

OPPOSITE ABOVE LEFT This ancient stone trough has been recycled as a rustic-style basin set on a bench-like support. The stone may have become worn with age, but that is part of its appeal.

OPPOSITE ABOVE RIGHT A huge chunk of roughly finished stone has a smoothly excavated centre and a highly polished top. The water spout is a slim pipe, cut on the diagonal.

OPPOSITE BELOW The rough exterior of a granite bowl contrasts with the smoothly polished interior to make a statement cloakroom basin.

'space-saving' toilets have the cistern and bowl closely joined, thus reducing the overall depth of the two. Then there are environmentally friendly dual-flush toilets (see page 52). Pressing the large button gives a six-litre (ten-and-a-half-pint) flush while the smaller uses only around three litres (five pints).

HYGIENE MATTERS

Several manufactures have developed hygienic, silicone-based, water-repellent, transparent glazes that are designed to repel limescale, dirt and water, and some companies are making toilet seats with antibacterial coatings. Another refinement is the advent of the soft-close seat and lid. This has a hinge mechanism that allows the lid and seat to glide smoothly back down to the closed position without needing to be handled.

Some companies have also addressed the problem of odours. A high-powered filter fitted near the lavatory waste pipe absorbs odour molecules

LEFT This slim, tapering basin pedestal is a modern take on a traditional idea.

BELOW LEFT An elegant double-basin combination incorporates colour and elements of design that are more often found in wooden furniture.

BELOW An oversized basin may take up less space than two separate ones, yet be just as capable of coping with two people's needs simultaneously.

A wall-hung lavatory and bidet combined in one unit looks streamlined and keeps the floor area free for easy cleaning.

BELOW BOTTOM Bidets and lavatories are usually sold in matching pairs.

BELOW RIGHT This bidet and lavatory duo are complemented by discreet taps and flush buttons that ensure the surrounding wall is easy to keep clean.

and is activated by a pressure-sensitive sensor installed in the lavatory seat which reacts to the weight of someone sitting on it.

BIDETS AND URINALS

Bidets and lavatories are usually bought as a matching pair and set side by side in the bathroom. Bidets are underrated pieces of equipment which offer benefits in terms of personal hygiene and comfort. They are also useful in homes where young children are in the early stages of toilet training and for elderly people who find taking a full bath or daily shower too difficult.

And finally, although urinals are most often found in commercial spaces, they can be used in a domestic setting and can help alleviate the pressure on toilet facilities in a male-dominated household. A urinal takes up a minimal amount of space and, with adequate plumbing, ventilation and a tiled surround and flooring, could even be accommodated in a small cloakroom or under a staircase.

TAPS

Although it is possible to mix and match tap styles in the bathroom it is important to keep them all in the same finish, in other words, all chrome, nickel or brass. It is also key to link the style of tap with the style of basin or bath. So, with an Art-Deco style bath, a traditional globe- or crystal-top chrome or nickel tap with faceted body and spout suits, while a modern glass basin is better with a streamlined spout and lever configuration.

Traditional taps, such as the cross-head with its ceramic discs for indicating hot and cold, usually come in pairs but contemporary designs often have a mixer spout and single control lever. Modern designers have tended to refine and simplify taps and spouts so they are now sleek and minimal and ergonomically designed to fit smoothly and neatly in the hand. Taps nowadays can be wall-mounted so they hang over the bath or basin, mounted on the side or back of a basin or bath, counter-mounted alongside a basin or, more often in the case of bath taps, floor-mounted.

ABOVE This type of lever tap was developed from those used in hospitals where the water is turned on by pushing the lever with the forearm rather than by turning by hand.

RIGHT A simple basin can be dressed up with smart taps. These heavy Art-Deco style tap-and-spout combinations accentuate the crisp, clean lines of the basins below.

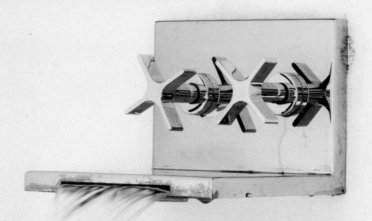

THIS PAGE This tap-and-spout combination makes a dramatic feature over a textured concrete bath. The shelf-like spout causes the water to fall in a flat cascade, while the white back panel unifies the bath and taps.

ABOVE RIGHT Lever taps can be beneficial for someone with arthritis or limited hand movement.

BELOW RIGHT Traditional cross-head taps have a timeless elegance, even in a modern bathroom.

BELOW Smooth-profile taps and spouts are easier to clean and polish than complex cross-head taps and more ornate designs.

BOTTOM CENTRE Wall-mounted taps free up the area around the basin. If they are positioned too high, the water will splash.

BOTTOM RIGHT The feather-like lever on top of this spout operates the on/off mechanism as well as controlling the water temperature.

LEFT Placing a radiator in front of a window will ensure that there is a 'wall' of warm air to counteract the coolness of the glass and air outside.

RIGHT In a good-size bathroom you may need only an extractor fan and the occasional opening of a window to expel steam and moisture. Low-level heating keeps the walls uncluttered.

BELOW A low-level heating source allows heat to rise but there is no risk of burning as there might be with a normal radiator.

HEAT & VENTILATION

A bathroom should be a warm and comfortable place to be when you are naked, but it is important that there no hot pipes or rails to burn yourself on. Radiators – and there are now some interesting designs on the market – may not be the only source of heat; they are often used in conjunction with heated towel rails or a radiator may incorporate a towel rail. If you have a separate heated towel rail, you may only need a small, low-level radiator. Underfloor heating is popular but it must be installed before the floor is laid so is mostly used in new-build or fully refurbished bathrooms.

Good ventilation is necessary to avoid the unpleasant effects of damp and condensation. These permeate towels, bath mats and shower curtains and also turn to water which collects in the bathroom's nooks and crannies. Here it causes mould and bacteria to flourish, which is not only unpleasant to look at but may also emit a dank odour. To counteract all this you need a good extractor fan or vent which brings cool fresh air into the room while removing the damp, moisture-laden air.

FAR LEFT Ladder-style radiators are popular, especially in small bathrooms, because they are slimline and go up, rather than along, the wall.

LEFT In this variation on a ladder radiator, the electric element runs the length of the central column, which also heats the 'rungs'.

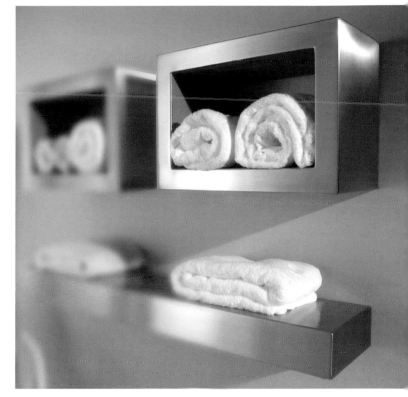

ABOVE These heated metal boxes keep hand towels and face cloths warm and well aired.

LEFT AND FAR LEFT These wall-mounted radiator panels have an integral towel rail. It is unwise to dry towels on or directly over night storage heaters or wall-mounted heaters because there is a risk of damaging the towels or, possibly, starting a fire.

MIRRORS

Mirrors play a functional role in the bathroom but they can be used to create illusion, too. A wall or large panel of mirror will reflect natural light, increasing its strength and giving the room a brighter, more invigorating feel. Mirrors also increase the strength of artificial light but can be arranged to create discreet highlights and a subtle glow if you want a more relaxed, mellow ambience.

A large expanse of mirror will give the bathroom an impression of greater depth and can be used to block out or disguise an irregular feature such as a disused chimney breast or an off-centre pillar.

Although most functional mirror is plain, there have been fashions for colours and tints to bring a feeling of opulence to even the simplest scheme. In the 1930s, peach-hued Champagne mirrors were in vogue; they add a soft warmth to the bathroom, while blue and green tints create a water-like impression and smoked or grey glass give an air of mystery and decadence.

ABOVE A mirrored panel creates the impression of space beyond, making the bathroom appear larger.

RIGHT An over-basin mirror lit by recessed strip lights will benefit from a concealed heating element to prevent the mirror from misting up.

OPPOSITE Adjustable angled panels of mirror give a perfect 360-degree view; they also reflect and magnify the natural light that comes from the bathroom window.

THIS PAGE Mirror panelling on a series of storage cupboard conceals their practical purpose and doubles the impact of the natural light.

TOP LEFT By extending the mirror below the basin, as well as above, the mirror becomes pillar-like and helps to accentuate the height of the space.

TOP RIGHT A curvy mirror creates an unexpected point of interest on this bathroom wall.

CENTRE LEFT This classic large-and-small mirror combination was created by Eileen Gray in the 1920s but is still popular today.

CENTRE RIGHT Hanging a light in front of a mirror will not only give you a clear view of yourself but will double the effect of the illumination.

BOTTOM LEFT By placing a mirror in front of the window, the daylight will shine on your face, rather than backlighting you, which would put your image in shadow.

BOTTOM RIGHT A mirror is incorporated into the sliding front of this sleek wall-mounted storage unit and is supplemented by a magnifying mirror on the countertop.

LIGHTING

ABOVE A strip of light
washes from the ceiling
down the front of the
sliding doors of a wall of
wardrobes. The plain
fronts of the cupboards
reflect some of the light
back into the bathroom.

RIGHT A subtle blue hue in
the lights concealed under
the deep shelves bring a
cool freshness to this
bathroom.

Ideally, a bathroom should have three levels of lighting. The
main, ambient light, to illuminate the whole room, may be provided by
halogen spotlights recessed in the ceiling. Secondary or task lighting is
needed to illuminate areas such as the mirror above the hand basin where
specific, directional light is required for shaving or applying make-up. This
type of light can be provided by an adjustable spotlight or by an encased strip
tube light. Thirdly, decorative lighting can be used to highlight features, add
colour or create a low-key, restful ambience. This lighting may be provided
by fibre optics or by wall-mounted fixtures with tinted bulbs and decorative
or coloured-glass shades.

If the ambient and task lighting are operated via a dimmer switch, then
they, too, can add to the decorative lighting effect in the room. By dimming

LEFT A warm-coloured feature light runs along the side of the bath. Its mellow glow softens the look of the concrete panelling and basins.

RIGHT Lampshades are generally undesirable in a bathroom but mounted away from splashes of water from the basin and with a wipeable shade, they can be attractive.

FAR RIGHT Strip lights alongside a large mirror are a reliable form of task lighting.

BELOW RIGHT Wall-mounted well above the basin, these lights will, for safety reasons, be turned on and off by a switch outside the bathroom.

the lights they will give a soft, low-level glow instead of fulfilling their usual functional role. But never have the light level so low that you cannot safely see how to get in and out of the bath or make your way across the room.

For safety, all bathroom lighting should be professionally installed and where it is in close contact with water, it should be in a sealed unit or casing. Light switches should be placed on the wall directly outside the bathroom. If they are inside, they should be operated by a pull cord so there is no danger of wet hands coming in direct contact with electricity.

Scented candles are frequently used for decorative lighting in bathrooms. Make sure they are safely placed in a holder or deep dish so the hot wax will not come into contact with your skin, and ensure that they are sited well away from towels, tissues, cotton wool, or any other flammable substances.

Fibre-optic lights are increasingly popular as a decorative feature in the bathroom. They can be laid through a ceiling to provide glittering, constellation-like clusters of twinkling light.

STORAGE

Three main types of storage are needed in a bathroom, one for bottles of cosmetic lotions and shampoos, another for cleaning agents and the third for items such as towels and face cloths and spare rolls of lavatory paper. Each type of storage has different requirements.

Cosmetics and shampoos should be easily accessible and sited close to the basin, shower and bath where they will be used. A good way of storing them is in a box or tray with a cloth in the base to soak up any drips. Storing them in one container also makes it easier to clean the surface on which they stand, as you only have to move one thing around rather a number.

Cleaning solutions such as bleach need to be stored safely, especially if

ABOVE Understated, high-tension steel cable with chrome fixings supports a series of glass shelves in a towel cupboard.

RIGHT This custom-made unit supports a finely honed stone basin but it also provides ample storage beneath with a series of drawers.

OPPOSITE Large wicker baskets contain all the necessary toiletries for washing that cannot be accommodated on the limited amount of space available on the basin surround.

LEFT This deep under-basin storage unit is faced with printed laminate whose intense graphic pattern conceals the joins of the drawers. The high-gloss surface is practical and easy to wipe clean.

BELOW A vintage drawer unit provides commodious storage and supports two stone basins. The basins and unit both have a simple rustic appeal.

children use the bathroom, in which case they should be in a locked cupboard or one with a tamper-proof catch. Medicines and first-aid requirements are often stored in the bathroom and, like cleaning agents, should be kept in a secure place. Toilet rolls, other paper products, spare towels and face cloths need to be stored somewhere dry, far away from contact with water and steam, in a warm cupboard or shelf.

Open shelves should be used sparingly because they attract dust and hairs and will therefore need frequent cleaning. Recessed niches are often used for displaying decorative items and books but may also

hold bottles and jars, although these are most practically stored in a bathroom cabinet above the basin or in a base unit or drawers underneath.

Your style of storage should complement the décor of your bathroom. In a contemporary scheme, built-in units in glass, metal, laminate or wood are in keeping. If, however, your style is more traditional, then an old armoire, chest of drawers or antique cabinet could be the answer – but make sure that the wood has a protective coat of paint or varnish and keep it away from direct contact with heat sources such as radiators, which might make the wood split.

WINDOW DRESSING

Bathroom windows present a dilemma because although you want as much natural light as possible, you also need privacy. And due to the dampness in a bathroom, you must ensure good ventilation and be able to open the window easily. Curtains pose another problem as the fabric absorbs moisture, which will make the curtains go limp and rot. They also collect dust and stray hairs, so they require regular, thorough cleaning.

The best window dressing for a bathroom is, therefore, a blind, of which there are very many types and styles. As well as being versatile enough to both screen and allow light in, it can be a decorative feature. What is more, blinds come in a wide variety of easy-to-clean materials and finishes.

ABOVE LEFT Blinds of roughly cut bamboo give a dappled light, and on these bottom-opening windows provides screening.

FAR LEFT Vertical blinds screen a tall window and emphasise the height of the room. They can be adjusted to vary the strength of light and the openness of the aspect.

LEFT Fine voile curtains need to be used in volume in order to create an effective screen.

RIGHT A hessian Roman blind is eye-catching and the dark band of colour helps provide privacy to the bather.

ABOVE A small window above a bath or basin can be screened with a decorative adhesive film. This is a quick and inexpensive window treatment that can easily be peeled off and replaced or updated.

LEFT If the outlook from your window is less than appealing, but the natural light is desirable, try a panel of semi-opaque tinted glass which will obscure the view without robbing you of daylight.

RIGHT ABOVE Sliding panels of semi-opaque fabric screen off the whole window but they can be used in a variety of combinations to give full or partial coverage.

Ways with windows

- If you have a sheer blind, fix a second blackout blind behind for nighttime.

- A quick and inexpensive way to keep out prying eyes is to paint the window glass with a dilute solution of white water-based paint.

- Don't need to cover the whole window? Then consider a half-curtain, upward-rolling blind or half height shutters.

The best source of illumination for any room is natural light. Not only does it give an exhilarating boost, but it is also free! To make the most of the available light in a bathroom you should avoid cluttering up the window with pelmets and curtains. Instead opt for blinds, acrylic resin panels, opaque or acid-etched glass or even adhesive vinyl attached to plain window glass. These can all fit neatly within the window frame so that they don't hang in the bath or interfere with taps or handles.

During daylight hours, semi-opaque window treatments provide privacy while allowing a gentle diffused light to penetrate the room but at night, when a light is on in the bathroom, take care. If you don't, your silhouette may well be seen from the outside.

RIGHT A coated fabric panel with a dappled patterned hangs from a narrow rail and fits neatly over the window surround, away from splashes of water and shampoo. If it does become wet, coated fabric like this can easily be patted dry.

Suppliers

BATHWARE SUPPLIERS

ALTERNATIVE PLANS
Tel: + 44 (0) 20 7243 9747
www.alternative-plans.co.uk

AQUAMASS S.A.
Tel: + 32 (0) 332 0732
www.aquamass.com

AMERICAN STANDARD
Tel: + 1-(800) 442-1902
www.americanstandard-us.com

ARMITAGE SHANKS
Tel: + 44 (0) 1543 490 253
www.armitage-shanks.co.uk

ASTON MATTHEWS
Tel: + 44 (0) 20 7226 7220
www.astonmatthews.co.uk

BATHROOM TECHNOLOGY LTD
Tel: + 44 (0) 7914 874 389
www.bathroomtechnology.co.uk

BATHROOMS INTERNATIONAL
Tel: + 44 (0) 20 7838 7788
www.bathroomsinternational.com

BATHSTORE
www.bathstore.com

BOFFI
Tel: + 1-(212) 431-8282
www.boffisoho.com

CASTELLO LUXURY BATHS LTD
Tel: + 44 (0) 1462 483 131
www.castellobaths.co.uk

CECO
Tel: + 1-(323) 588-8108
www.cecosinks.com

CLAWFOOT SUPPLY
Tel: + 1-(877) 682-4192
www.clawfootsupply.com

COLOURWASH
Tel: + 44 (0) 20 8944 2695
www.colourwash.co.uk

CZECH & SPEAKE
Tel: + 44 (0) 20 7439 0216
www.czechspeake.co.uk

DURAVIT UK LTD
Tel: + 44 (0) 870 730 7787
www.duravit.co.uk

EBB SPACE
Tel: + 44 (0) 283 752 3735
www.ebbspace.com

GEBERIT LTD
Tel: + 44 (0) 1622 717 811
www.geberit.co.uk

C. P. HART
www.cphart.co.uk

HERITAGE BATHROOMS
Tel: + 44 (0) 117 963 3333
www.heritagebathrooms.com

H$_2$O LONDON
Tel: + 44 (0) 20 7720 3618
www.h2olondon.com

IDEAL STANDARD (UK) LTD
Tel: + 44 (0) 1482 346461
www.ideal-standard.co.uk

IMPERIAL WARE
Tel: + 44 (0) 121 328 6824
www.imperial-ware.com

JACUZZI UK
Tel: + 44 (0) 1782 717 175
www.jacuzzi.co.uk

JUST ADD WATER
Tel: + 44 (0) 20 7697 3161
www.justaddwater.co.uk

KOHLER
Tel: + 1-(800) 4-KOHLER
www.kohler.com

LAUFEN
Tel: + 44 (0) 1386 422 768
www.laufen.co.uk

MANSFIELD
Tel: + 1-(419) 938-5211
www.mansfieldplumbing.com

ORIGINAL BATHROOMS
Tel: + 44 (0) 20 8940 7554
www.original-bathrooms.co.uk

PORCELANOSA
Tel: + 44 (0) 800 915 4000
(brochure line)
www.porcelanosa.co.uk

QUALCERAM
Tel: + 35 (0) 340 231 288
www.qualceram-shires.com

ROCA LTD
Tel: + 44 (0) 1530 830 080
www.roca-uk.com

SOPHA INDUSTRIES
Tel: + 33 (0) 142 812 585
www.sopha.fr

TEUCO
Tel: + 44 (0) 20 7704 2190
www.teuco.co.uk

TILES & BATHS DIRECT
Tel: + 44 (0) 20 8202 2223
www.tilesandbathsdirect.co.uk

TWYFORD BATHROOMS
Tel: + 44 (0) 1270 879 777
www.twyfordbathrooms.com

VILLEROY & BOCH
Tel: + 44 (0) 10 8871 4028
www.villeroy-boch.com

VITRA
Tel: + 44 (0) 1235 750 990
www.vitrauk.com

THE WATER MONOPOLY
Tel: + 44 (0) 20 7624 2636
www.watermonopoly.com

WATERWORKS
Tel: + 1-(800) 899-6757
www.waterworks.com

WEST ONE BATHROOMS
Tel: + 44 (0) 20 7499 1845
www.westonebathrooms.com

WHIRLPOOL SPA LTD
Tel: + 44 (0) 1527 594 202
info@whirlpoolspa.co.uk

THE YARD
Tel: + 44 (0) 28 9040 5600
www.theyard.co.uk

SHOWER HEADS

AQUALISA PRODUCTS LTD
Tel: + 44 (0) 1959 560 020
www.aqualisa.co.uk.

AQUAPLUS SOLUTIONS LTD
Tel: + 44 (0) 845 201 1915
www.aquaplussolutions.com

CROSSWATER LTD
Tel: + 44 (0) 1322 628 270
www.crosswater.co.uk

DORNBRACHT
Tel: + 44 (0) 2476 717 129
www.dornbracht.com

GROHE
www.grohe.com

MATKI PLC
Tel: + 44 (0) 1454 322 888
www.matki.co.uk

MIRA
Tel: + 44 (0) 845 600 6472
www.mirashowers.co.uk

ROMAN SHOWERS
Tel: + 44 (0) 1325 311 318
www.roman-showers.com

SHOWERLUX U.K. LTD
Tel: + 44 (0) 2476 639 400
www.showerlux.uk.com

TRITON PLC
Tel: + 44 (0) 24 7634 4441
www.tritonshowers.co.uk

VOLA
Tel: + 44 (0) 1525 841 155
www.vola.co.uk

CONTEMPORARY TAPS AND MIXERS

BRISTAN LTD
Tel: + 44 (0) 870 4425 555
www.bristan.com

DORNBRACHT (see Shower Heads)

DAVROC LTD
Tel: + 44 (0) 1992 441 672
www.davroc.co.uk

GROHE
(see Shower Heads)

HANSGROHE LTD
Tel: + 44 (0) 870 770 1972
www.hansgrohe.co.uk

JADO LTD
Tel: + 44 (0) 800 380 923
www.jado-uk.com

MATKI PLC
(see Shower Heads)

PEGLER LTD
Tel: + 44 (0) 870 1200 284
(brochure request)
www.pegler.co.uk

PERRIN & ROWE
Tel: + 44 (0) 1708 526 361
www.perrinandrowe.co.uk

SERDANELI INTERNATIONAL
Tel: + 33 (0) 141 701 70
www.serdaneli-international.com

SWADLING BRASSWARE
Tel: + 44 (0) 1454322888
www.swadlingbrassware.com

WINDOW TREATMENTS

FABER BLINDS
Tel: + 44 (0) 1604 766251
www.faberblinds.co.uk

HILLARYS
Blinds (+ 44 (0) 800 916 6524)
and American-style wooden
louvre shutters
(+ 44 (0) 800 916 7713)
www.hillarys.co.uk

LEAD & LIGHT
Tel: + 44 (0) 20 7485 0997
www.leadandlight.co.uk

NEW HOUSE TEXTILES
Tel: + 44 (0) 1989 740 684
www.newhousetextiles.com

NOVATEC
Tel: + 44 (0) 1843 850 666

RUFLETTE LTD
Tel: + 44 (0) 161 998 1811
www.rufflette.com

SALT
Tel: + 44 (0) 20 7593 0007
www.salt-uk.com

SANDERSON
Tel: + 44 (0) 1895 830 044
www.sanderson-uk.com

SHAFTESBURY SHUTTERS
Tel: + 44 (0) 845 166 4103
www.shaftesburyshutters.co.uk

SHY UK
Tel: + 44 (0) 845 6720 000
www.shy.co.uk

SILENT GLISS LTD
Tel: + 44 (0) 1843 863 571
www.silentgliss.co.uk

SURFACE MATERIAL DESIGN
Tel: + 44 (0) 20 8671 3383
www.surfacematerialdesign.co.uk

WEB-BLINDS.COM
Tel: + 44 (0) 800 169 3938
www.web-blinds.com

FURNITURE AND ARCHITECTURAL FEATURES

ARAM DESIGNS
Tel: + 44 (0) 20 7557 7557
www.aram.co.uk

THE CONRAN SHOP
Tel: + 44 (0) 20 7589 7401
www.conran.com

DOMUS
Tel: + 44 (0) 20 8525 0682
www.domusfurniture.co.uk

EM-B SOLUTIONS LTD
Tel : + 44 (0) 113 245 9559
www.em-b.co.uk

GIBSON MUSIC
Tel: + 44 (0) 20 7384 2270
www.gibson-music.com

GOODWOOD BATHROOMS
Tel: + 44 (0) 1243 532 121
www.goodwoodbathrooms.co.uk

HABITAT
www.habitat.net

HEAL'S
Tel: + 44 (0) 20 7636 1666
www.heals.co.uk

IKEA
www.ikea.com

SCP
Tel: + 44 (0) 20 7739 1869
www.scp.co.uk

SHADES FURNITURE
Tel: + 44 (0) 1937 842 394
www.shadesfurniture.co.uk

WATERLINE LTD
Tel: + 44 (0) 870 556 1560
www.waterline.co.uk

THE WATER MONOPOLY
(see Bathroom Suppliers)

ACCESSORIES

AIRFLOW DEVELOPMENTS LTD
Tel: + 44 (0) 1494 525 252
www.iconfan.co.uk

ALESSI
Tel: + 44 (0) 20 7518 909
www.alessi.com

AQUAVISION TV
Tel: + 44 (0) 1992 708 333
www.aquavision.tv

BED, BATH & BEYOND
Tel: + 1-(800) 0462-3966
www.bedbath.com

BLISS
Tel: + 44 (0) 1789 400 077
www.blisshome.co.uk

BRISTAN LTD (see
Contemporary Taps and Mixers)

EDMUND DE WAAL
Tel: + 44 (0) 20 8674 1122
www.edmunddewaal.com

THE HOLDING COMPANY
Tel: + 44 (0) 20 7352 1600
www.theholdingcompany.co.uk

MIRROR MEDIA LTD
Tel: + 44 (0) 870 3866 333
www.mirrormedia.com

MUJI
Tel: + 44 (0) 20 7437 7503
www.mujionline.co.uk

PHFACTOR
Tel: + 44 (0) 20 7483 3639
www.phfactor.co.uk

PHILIPS
www.philips.com

PORTER LANCASTRIAN LTD
Tel: + 44 (0) 870 871 0113
www.porta.co.uk

TECHNOGYM UK LTD
Tel: + 44 (0) 1344 300 236
www.technogym.co.uk

WET ROOMS, STEAM AND SHOWER ENCLOSURES

BOUNDARY BATHROOMS
Tel: + 44 (0) 845 009 9545
www.boundarybathrooms.co.uk

DESIGN REPUBLIC LTD
Tel: + 44 (0) 1638 676 750
www.design-republic.net

DURAVIT UK LTD (see Bathware Suppliers)

HSK
Tel: + 44 (0) 1889 564 030
www.hsk-showers.com

IMPEY UK LTD
Tel: + 44 (0) 1460 256 080
www.impey-uk.com

JACUZZI UK (see Bathware Suppliers)

KOHLER DARYL LTD
Tel: + 44 (0) 151 606 5000
www.daryl-showers.co.uk

SAMUEL HEATH
Tel: + 44 (0) 121 772 2303
www.samuel-heath.com

SCULPTURED HOMES
Tel: + 1-(877) WET-SPAS
www.sculpturedhomes.com

RADIATORS

FEATURE RADIATORS LTD
Tel: + 44 (0) 1274 567789
www.featureradiators.com

MHS RADIATORS
Tel: + 44 (0) 1268 546 700
www.mhsradiators.com

MODULAR HEATING GROUP
Tel: + 44 (0) 1268 546700
www.mhsradiators.com

MYSON RADIATORS
Tel: + 44 (0) 845 4023 434
www.myson.co.uk

LIGHTING

ARTEMIDE
www.artemide.com

AURORA LTD
Tel: + 44 (0) 870 444 1106
www.aurora.eu.com

JOHN CULLEN LIGHTING
Tel: + 44 (0) 20 7371 5400
www.johncullenlighting.co.uk

LIGHT IQ
Tel: + 44 (0) 20 8749 1900
www.lightiq.com

LIGHT-MY-HOUSE
Tel: + 44 (0) 1732 897 820
www.light-my-house.co.uk

THE LONDON LIGHTING COMPANY
Tel: + 44 (0) 20 7589 3612

LUCHO BRIEVA
Tel: + 44 (0) 20 8960 2794
www.luchobrieva.com

LUTRON EA LTD
Tel: + 44 (0) 20 7702 0657
www.lutron.com

MR LIGHT
Tel: + 44 (0) 20 7352 8398
www.mrlight.co.uk

NU-LINE
Tel: + 44 (0) 20 7727 7748
www.nu-line.net

SKK
Tel: + 44 (0) 20 7434 4095
www.skk.net

HEATED MIRRORS

SATANA INTERNATIONAL LTD
Tel: + 44 (0) 1935 891 888
www.heatedmirrors.co.uk

FLOORS AND WALLS

ABET LAMINATES
Tel: + 44 (0) 20 7473 6910
www.abet-ltd.com

AMTICO
Tel: + 44 (0) 121 745 0800
www.amtico.com

ARCHITECTURAL CERAMICS
Tel: + 44 (0) 121 706 6456
www.actiles.co.uk

CORIAN
Tel: + 44 (0) 800 962 116
www.corian.com

DALSOUPLE RUBBER
Tel: + 44 (0) 1278 727 733
www.dalsouple.com

DOMINIC CRINSON
Tel: + 44 (0) 20 7613 2783
www.crinson.com

DOMUS
Tel: + 44 (0) 20 8481 9500
www.domustiles.com

FIRED EARTH
Tel: + 44 (0) 1295 812 088
www.firedearth.com

FIRST FLOOR
Tel: + 44 (0) 20 7736 1123
www.firstfloor.uk.com

FORMICA LTD UK
Tel: + 44 (0) 191 259 3000
www.formica.co.uk

ISLAND STONE
Tel: + 44 (0) 800 083 9351
www.islandstone.co.uk

MARCA CORONA
www.marcacorona.it

MARGRASIL UK LTD
Tel: + 44 (0) 852352
www.margrasil.co.uk

PANDA FLOORING COMPANY
Tel: + 44 (0) 116 242 4816
www.pandaflooring.co.uk

PARIS CERAMICS
Tel: + 44 (0) 20 7371 7778
www.parisceramics.com

PENTAGON TILES
Tel: + 44 (0) 1279 62662
www.pentagon-tiles.co.uk

PILKINGTON GROUP LTD
Tel: + 44 (0) 1744 28882
www.pilkington.co.uk

REED HARRIS TILES
Tel: + 44 (0) 20 7736 7511
www.reedharris.co.uk

THE RUBBER FLOORING COMPANY
Tel: + 44 (0) 800 849 6386
www.therubberflooringcompany.co.uk

SLATE WORLD
Tel: + 44 (0) 20 8204 3444
www.slateworld.com

STONE AGE
Tel: + 44 (0) 207 384 9090
www.stone-age.co.uk

STONEHOUSE
Tel: + 44 (0) 800 093 9724
www.stonehousetiles.co.uk

TOPPS TILES
Tel: + 44 (0) 800 783 6262
www.toppstiles.co.uk

UK MARBLE
Tel: + 44 (0) 1432 352 112
www.ukmarble.co.uk

WORLD'S END TILES
Tel: + 44 (0) 20 7819 2100
www.worldsendtiles.co.uk

TILE TRANSFERS

UGLY EDITIONS
Tel: + 33 (0) 620 61 37
www.ugly-home.com

GENERAL CONTACTS

ASSOCIATION OF PLUMBING
AND HEATING CONTRACTORS
Tel: + 44 (0) 24 7647 0626
www.aphc.co.uk

BATHROOM MANUFACTURERS
ASSOCIATION
Tel: + 44 (0) 1782 747123
www.bathroom-association.org

CONFEDERATION FOR THE
REGISTRATION OF GAS
INSTALLERS (CORGI)
Tel: + 44 (0) 870 401 2300
www.corgi-gas-safety.com

INSTITUTE OF PLUMBING AND
HEATING ENGINEERING
Tel: + 44 (0) 870 414 5533
www.iphe.org.uk

NATIONAL INSPECTION
COUNCIL FOR ELECTRICAL
INSTALLATION CONTRACTING
Tel: + 44 (0) 870 013 0382
www.niceic.org.uk

NLG ASSOCIATES
Tel: + 44 (0) 20 7253 0358
www.nlgassociates.co.uk

OFWAT
Tel: + 44 (0) 121 625 1300 / 1373
www.ofwat.gov.uk

ROYAL INSTITUTE OF BRITISH
ARCHITECTS (RIBA)
BOOKSHOPS
Tel: + 44 (0) 20 7256 7222
www.ribabookshops.com

Architects & Designers

1100 ARCHITECT
435 Hudson Street
New York New York 10014
USA
Tel: + 1-(212) 645-1011
www.1100architect.com

AGNÈS EMERY
12 rue de Lausanne
10060 Brussels Belgium
Tel: + 32 (0) 2 538 2134
www.emeryetcie.com

ANDERSON MASON DALE
ARCHITECTS
1615 Seventeenth Street
Denver Colorado 80202
USA
Tel: + 1-(303) 294-9448
www.amdarchitects.com

ANDREA TRUGLIO
75 via del Corso
00186 Rome Italy
Tel: + 39 (0) 6 361 1836

ANDRÉE PUTMAN
83 avenue Denfert-Rochereau
75014 Paris France
Tel: + 33 (0) 1 55 42 88 55
www.andreeputman.com

ANTHONY HUDSON
Hudson Architects
49-59 Old Street
London EC1V 9HX
Tel: + 44 (0) 20 7490 3411
www.hudsonarchitects.co.uk

ARCHITECTUS
Patrick Clifford
1 Centre Street PO Box 90621
AMSC Freemans Bay
Auckland New Zealand
Tel: + 64 (0) 9 307 5970
www.architectus.com.au

AXEL VERVOORDT
Kasteel van 's-Gravenwezel
Sint Jobsttenweg 64
2970 's-Gravenwezel Belgium
Tel: + 32 (0) 3 355 33 00
www.axel-vervoordt.com

BLACK KOSLOFF KNOTT
ARCHITECTS
Level 9 180 Russell Street
Melbourne Victoria 3000
Australia
Tel: + 61 (0) 3 9671 4555
www.b-k-k.com.au

BOOTH HANSEN ASSOCIATES
Laurence Booth
555 South Dearborn Street
Chicago Illinois 60605
USA
Tel: + 1-(312) 427-0300
www.boothhansen.com

BRUCE BIERMAN DESIGN INC
29 West 15th Street
New York New York 10011
USA
Tel: + 1-(212) 243-1935
www.biermandesign.com

CHARLES RUTHERFOORD
51 The Chase London SW4 0NP
Tel: + 44 (0) 20 7627 0182
www.charlesrutherfoord.net

CLINTON MURRAY
ARCHITECTS
2 King Street Merimbula
New South Wales 2548
Australia
Tel: + 61 (0) 2 6495 1954
www.clintonmurray.com.au

CLODAGH DESIGN
Tel: + 1-(212) 780-5755
www.clodagh.com

COLLETT-ZARZYCKI
ARCHITECTS & DESIGNERS
Fernhead Studios
2b Fernhead Road London W9 3ET
Tel: + 44 (0) 20 8969 6967
www.collett-zarzycki.com

CURTIS WOOD ARCHITECTS
23-28 Penn Street
London N1 5DL
Tel: + 44 (0) 20 7684 1400
www.curtiswoodarchitects.com

ÉRIC GIZARD ASSOCIÉS
14 rue Crespin du Gast
75001 Paris France
Tel: + 33 (0) 1 55 28 38 58
www.gizardassocies.com

FOUGERON ARCHITECTURE
431 Tehama Street
Suite 1 San Francisco
California 94103 USA
Tel: + 1-(415) 641-5744
www.fougeron.com

FRANÇOIS MARCQ
8 rue Fernand Neuray
1050 Brussels Belgium
Tel: + 32 (0) 2 513 1328

FRED COLLIN
Dransdale Lodge
York YO62 7JL
Tel: + 44 (0) 1751 431137

FRÉDÉRIC MÉCHICHE
14 rue Saint Croix de la Bretonnerie
75004 Paris France
Tel: + 33 (0) 1 42 78 78 28

FUSION DESIGN & ARCHITECTURE
4 Risborough Street
London SE1 0HE
Tel: + 44 (0) 20 7928 9982
www.fusiondna.b4-design.com

GALERIE YVES GASTOU
12 rue Bonaparte
75006 Paris France
Tel: + 33 (0) 1 53 73 00 10
www.galerieyvesgastou.com

GILLES PELLERIN
Collection Privée
9 rue des États-Unis
06400 Cannes France
Tel: + 33 (0) 4 97 06 94 94
www.collection-privee.com

HELENE FORBES-HENNIE
Hennie Interiors Thomlesgt 4
0270 Oslo Norway
Tel: + 47 22 06 85 86

HOLLY LUEDERS
36 East 72nd Street
New York New York 10021 USA
Tel: + 1-(212) 535-6651

JAMES GORST ARCHITECTS
The House of Detention
Clerkenwell Close
London EC1R 0AS
Tel: + 44 (0) 7336 7140
www.jamesgorstarchitects.com

JEAN-DOMINIQUE BONHOTAL
12 rue Alfred de Vigny
75008 Paris France
Tel: + 33 (0) 1 56 79 10 80

JEAN-MARC VYNCKIER
49 rue Daubenton
59100 Roubaix France
Tel: + 33 (0) 3 20 27 86 59

JOHANN SLEE
Slee Architects & Interiors 32
Pallinghurst Road
Westcliff 2193 South Africa
Tel: + 27 (0) 11 646 9935
johann@slee.co.za

KARIM EL ACHAK ARCHITECT
7 rue de la Liberté
Marrakech Morroco
Tel: + 212 (0) 44 44 73 13
associati@menara.ma

KARIM RASHID INC
357 West 17th Street
New York New York 10011 USA
Tel: + 1-(212) 929-8657
www.karimrashid.com

KELLY HOPPEN INTERIORS
2 Munden Street
London W14 0RH
Tel: + 44 (0) 20 7471 3350
www.kellyhoppen.com

KRISTIINA RATIA DESIGNS
Tel: + 1-(202) 852-0027
kristiinaratia@aol.com

LENA PROUDLOCK
4 The Chipping Tetbury
Gloucestershire GL8 8ET
Tel: + 44 (0) 166 500051
www.lenaproudlock.com

LEONARDO CHALUPOWICZ
3527 Landa Street
Los Angeles
California 90039
USA
Tel: + 1-(323) 660-8261
www.chalupowicz.com

LES ÉDITIONS DOMINIQUE
KIEFFER
8 rue Herold
75001 Paris France
Tel: + 33 (0) 1 42 212 32 44
www.dkieffer.com

MAX LAWRENCE
264 Douar Ouled Ben Rahmoun
Marrakech Palmeraie
Morocco
Tel: + 2 (0) 12 24 30 03 02
info@caravanserai.com

MICHAEL TRAPP
7 River Road
Box 67 West Cornwall
Connecticut 06796 USA
Tel: + 1-(860) 672-6098

NANCY BRAITHWAITE
INTERIORS
1198 Howell Mill Road NW
Suite 110
Atlanta Georgia 30318
USA
Tel: + 1-(404) 355-1740
www.bbraithwaite.com

NEXT ARCHITECTS
Weesperzijde 93
1091 EK Amsterdam
The Netherlands
Tel: + 31 (0) 20 463 0463
www.nextarchitects.com

PAMPLEMOUSSE DESIGN INC
12 Charles Street
Suite 6D
New York New York 10014
USA
Tel: + 1-(212) 741-0073
www.pamplemoussedesign.com

PAOLO BADESCO
Viale di Porta Vercellina 5
20123 Milan Italy
Tel: + 39 (0) 24 100 737
www.paolobadesco.it

RAMÓN ESTEVE ARCHITECTS
Estudio de Arquitectura
Jorge Juan 8, 5°, 11a
46004 Valencia Spain
Tel: + 34 96 351 04 34
www.ramonesteve.com

RIOS CLEMENTI HALE
STUDIOS
6824 Melrose Avenue
Los Angeles
California 90038
USA
Tel: + 1-(323) 634-9220
www.rios.com

SEIBERT ARCHITECTS PA
325 Central Avenue
Sarasota
Florida 34236
USA
Tel: + 1-(941) 366-9151
www.seibertarchitects.com

SELLDORF ARCHITECTS
62 White Street
New York
New York 10012
USA
Tel: + 1-(212) 219-9571
www.selldorf.com

SETH STEIN ARCHITECTS
15 Grand Union Centre
West Row Ladbroke Grove
London W10 5AS
Tel: + 44 (0) 20 8968 8581
www.sethstein.com

SILVIO RECH & LESLEY
CARSTENS
Architecture & Interior
Architecture
Tel: + 27 (0) 829 009935
adventarch@mweb.co.za

SOLIS BETANCOURT
1739 Connecticut Avenue NW
Washington
DC 20009
USA
Tel: + 1-(202) 659-8734
www.solisbetancourt.com

STEPHANIE HOPPEN
17 Walton Street
London SW3 2HX
Tel: + 44 (0) 20 7589 3678
www.stephaniehoppen.com

STEVEN EHRLICH FAIA
10865 Washington Boulevard
Culver City
California 90232
USA
Tel: + 1-(310) 838-9700
www.s-ehrlich.com

TERRY HUNZIGER INC
208 3rd Avenue South
Seattle
Washington 98104
USA
Tel: + 1-(206) 467-1144

THOMAS KJAERHOLM
Rungstedvej 86
2960 Rungsted Kyst
Denmark
Tel: + 45 (0) 45 76 56 56
www.kjaerholms.dk

Acknowledgements

Photographers' credits

Ken Hayden 30-31, 48 right, 54-55, 60-61, 107, 108 below right, 117 centre, 125 above right & 129 above left.
Vincent Knapp 4, 23, 46, 58, 71 below, 72-73, 94, 98 right, 108 below left, 109, 122 below, 126-127, 130 above.
Ray Main/Mainstreamimages 27, 49, 70, 78-79, 99 & 116.
Photozest/Inside/B Claessens 26 below.
Lucinda Symons 1, 18-19, 48 left, 92 above & 125 centre left.
Simon Upton 6 below, 11 above right, 13, 14, 15 above, 18 right, 22 left, 28, 29, 30, 34 above, 36-37, 40-41, 51 above, 57 below right, 75 above, 76 above, 77, 82-83, 90 above left, 90 above right, 91, 96, 97 above left, 97 below left, 97 right, 102 above, 108 above right,110, 122 above, 129 below, 131 & 114-145.
Frederic Vasseur 7, 12 left, 24, 36 above 45 left & 53 right.
Fritz von der Schulenberg 50, 76 below, 135 & 137 right.
Andreas von Einsiedel 52.
Luke White 16-17, 89 below.
Andrew Wood 2, 3, 5, 6 above, 8-9, 11, 15 below, 16, 18 left, 20-21, 22 right, 25, 26 above, 32, 33 above, 34 below, 35, 39, 40-41, 42-43, 44, 45 right, 47, 51 below, 57 below, 59, 62, 63 above, 63 below, 64 right, 72, 74, 75 below, 76 above, 81 right, 87, 88, 89 above, 93, 100, 101, 102 below, 103, 106,108 centre, 111 above right, 111 below, 113 below left, 113 below right, 114, 117 below left, 117 below right, 119, 123, 125 centre right, 125 below left, 125 below right, 128, 129 above, 132, 134 above, 134 below right & 136 left.

Suppliers' credits

1 accessories by Roca; 48 left Reed Harris Tiles; 52 Gibson Music; 64 above left Aston Mattthews; 64 below left Sopha Industries/Collection Wet; 65 Dominic Crinson; 66 Sopha Industries/Collection Outline; 67 above Aston Matthews; 67 below Sopha Industries/Collection Wet; 68 Ebb Space; 68-69 MCGM; 71 above West One Bathrooms; 80 Ian Hogarth; 81 left Sopha Industries/Collection Wet; 85 above left Aquaplus Solutions; 85 above right MHS RADIATORS; 85 below left Sopha Industries; 85 below right MHS RADIATORS; 90 below left Dominic Crinson; 92 above Edmund de Waal ceramics; 95 above left Sopha Industries/Collection Artiquitect Hayon; 95 above right Publicity Engineers/C P Hart/Istanbul Collection; 95 below Le Sok; 98 left Bathrooms International; 104 above right The Yard/Chiocciola; 104 left MCGM/Arabia; 104 below rightThe Yard/Kos; 105 above left Publicity Engineers/CP Hart/Istanbul Collection; 105 below Sopha Industries/Collection Wet; 105 below centre Swaddling Taps; 105 right Sopha Industries/Vola Collection; 108 Althea Wilson; 112 above Publicity Engineers/C P Hart/Istanbul Collection; 112 below left Sopha Industries/ Collection Artquitect Hayon; 112 below right Sopha Industries/Collection Wet; 113 above Sopha Industries /Kisses Collection; 113 centre left Ideal Standard; 113 below left Aquaplus Solutions; 113 below right Aquaplus Solutions; 115 Citterrio; 118 MHS RADIATORS; 120 left MHS RADIATORS; 121 MHS RADIATORS; 136 right Surface Material Design.

Location credits

2 Jasper Conran's home in London; 3 left a house in Johannesburg, designed by Johann Slee; 3 centre Michael Trapp's house in Connecticut; 3 right a house in Italy designed by Paolo Badesco; 4 designer Kelly Hoppen; 5 Richard & Lucille Lewin's house in London, designed by Seth Stein; 6 above Mark Rios' home in Los Angeles; 6 below Ivy Ross & Brian Gill's home in Galisteo; 7 Reed & Delphine Krakoff's Manhattan townhouse, designed by Pamplemousse Design Inc.; 8-9 an apartment in Belgium, designed by François Marcq; 11 above left an apartment in Paris, designed by Frédéric Méchiché; 11 above right a mountain retreat in Colorado, designed by Ron Mason; 11 below left Silvio Rech & Lesley Carstens' house near Johannesburg; 11 below right Fougeron Architecture; 12 left Patrizio Fradianis' house in Chicago, designed by Patrizio Fradiani at Studio F; 13 Loft-style conversion in London, designed by Ushida Findlay architects; 14 Ivy Ross & Brian Gill's home in Galisteo; 15 below Mark Rios' home in Los Angeles; 16 Seibert Architects; 16-17 a New York penthouse loft designed by Clodagh Design; 18 left De Stad residence, Amsterdam designed by Next Architects; 18 right Tigmi, Morocco, designed by Max Lawrence; 18-19 Matthew Drennan and Hamish McArdle's house in London; 20-21 Fourgeron Architecture; 22 left Wingate Jackson, Jr and Paul Trantanella's house in upstate New York; 22 right Keith & Cathy Abell's New York house, designed by 1100 Architect; 23 designer Kelly Hoppen; 24 Charles Rutherfoord & Rupert Tyler's London flat; 25 below Weaving/Thomasson residence, Essex; 26 above a house in Johannesburg, designed by Johann Slee; 28 Agnès Emery's house in Marrakech; 29 a house in Virginia designed by Solis Betancourt; 30 a house in Oxfordshire designed by Todhunter Earle; 30-31 Patrick de Poortere's apartment, designed by Andrée Putman; 32 a house in New South Wales designed by Clinton Murray; 33 above an apartment in Paris designed by Studio KO; 34 above Mr & Mrs Stokke's cabin in the Norwegian mountains, interior design by Helene Forbes-Hennie; 34 below Weaving/Thomasson residence, Essex; 35 Interiors by Wilson Stiles, Sarasota, Florida; 36 above a house in Suffolk designed by James Gorst; 36 below Axel Vervoodt's house in Belgium; 36-37 Agnès Emery's house in Brussels; 38 Halpern PR/Taylor Howes Designs; 39 left a house near Grasse, France, designed by Collett-Zarzycki Architects & Designers; 39 right Karim El Achak's house in Marrakech; 40 Karim El Achak's house in Marrakech; 40-41 Architect Gilles Pellerin's house in Cannes; 42-43 a house near Cape Town designed by Johann Slee; 44 a house in Victoria, Australia designed by Black Kosloff Knott; 45 left a house in Suffolk designed by James Gorst; 45 right a house in New South Wales designed by Clinton Murray; 46 designer Kelly Hoppen; 47 left a penthouse loft in New York,

designed by Bruce Bierman Design Inc.; 47 right Kristiina Ratia's Connecticut home; 48 right Patrick de Portere's apartment, designed by Andrée Putman; 50 designer Nancy Braithwaite; 51 above Hanne Kjaerholm's house in Copenhagen; 51 below an apartment in Belgium, designed by François Marcq; 53 right Lena Proudlock's house in Gloucestershire; 54-55 Susan & Paul Zucker's Chicago home, designed by Larry Booth; 57 Andrea Truglio's apartment in Rome; 57 below left Silvio Rech & Lesley Carstens' house near Johannesburg; 57 below right an apartment in Paris designed by Frédéric Méchiche; 58 designer Kelly Hoppen; 59 an apartment in Brussels, designed by Vincent Van Duysen; 60-61 Jackie Villevoye's house in the Netherlands; 62 a house in Ibiza designed by Ramón Esteve Architects; 63 a house in Italy designed by Paolo Badesco; 64 right designer Fred Collin; 71 below designer Kelly Hoppen; 72 Stark residence, London, designed by Curtis Wood Architects; 72-73 designer Kelly Hoppen; 74 Silvio Rech & Lesley Carstens' house near Johannesburg; 75 above a cabin in Aspen, designed by Holly Lueders; 75 below Paolo Badesco's villa in Italy; 76 above an apartment in Paris designed by Frédéric Méchiche; 77 Stephanie Hoppen's London house; 81 right Jean-Marc Vynckier's home in Lille; 82-83 Peter & Marijke de Wit of Domaine d'Heerstaayen in the Netherlands; 87 a house in Tuscon, Arizona, design by Voorsanger & Associates; 88 Johann Slee's home in Johannesburg; 89 above Peter Wheeler & Pascale Revert's London home, designed by Eric Gizard; 89 below a New York penthouse loft designed by Clodagh Design; 90 above left Agnès Emery's house in Marrakech; 90 above right a house in London designed by Frédéric Mechiche; 91 James Gager & Richard Ferretti's Pennsylvanian house; 93 a house in Ibiza designed by Ramón Esteve; 96 a house in France decorated by Yves Gastou; 97 below left Alastair Gordon & Barbara de Vries' New Jersey home; 97 right Dominique Kieffer's house in Normandy; 98 right designer Kelly Hoppen; 100 Stark Residence, London designed by Curtis Wood Architects; 101 above Patrick Clifford's house in Auckland designed by Architectus; 101 below Susanna Colleoni & Didi Huber's home in Milan; 102 above Agnès Emery's house in Marrakech; 102 below Karim El Achak's house in Marrakech; 103 a house in Marrakech designed by Karl Fournier & Olivier Marty, Studio KO; 106 a house in Ibiza, designed by Ramón Esteve Architects; 107 Jean-Dominique Bonhotal's apartment; 108 above left designer Althea Wilson; 108 above right a Paris apartment designed by Frederic Mechiche; 108 centre left interior design by Angi Lincoln; 108 centre right Pam SKaist Levy's Hollywood Hills house, designed by Leonardo Chalupowicz; 108 below left designer Kelly Hoppen; 108 below right designed by Terry Hunziker; 109 designer Kelly Hoppen; 110 Tigmi, Morocco, designed by Max Lawrence; 111 above right Keith & Cathy Abell's New York house designed by 1100 Architect; 111 below Steven Ehrlich, FAIA's house in Venice, California; 114 left Jean-Marc Vynckier's home in Lille; 117 centre designed by Terry Hunziker;

117 below left an apartment in Brussels designed by Vincent van Duysen; 117 below centre Jean-Marc Vynckier's home in Lille ; 117 below right an apartment in Belgium designed by François Marcq; 119 a house in East Hampton designed by Selldorf Architects; 120 right a house in Guernsey, designed by James Falla at MOOArc; 122 above Agnès Emery's house in Marrakech; 122 below designer Kelly Hoppen; 123 Peter Wheeler & Pascale Revert's London home, designed by Eric Gizard; 125 above left what project; 125 above right designed by Terry Hunziker; 125 centre left Edmund de Waal ceramic vases; 125 centre right Eric Gizard's apartment in Paris; 125 below left James Mohn and Keith Recker's apartment in New York; 125 below right Stark Residence, London designed by Curtis Wood Architects; 126-127 designer Kelly Hoppen; 128 Richard & Lucille Lewin's house in London designed by Seth Stein; 129 above left bathroom designed by Sally Sirkin Lewis; 129 above right Sophie Douglas of Fusion Design & Architecture's converted barn in Somerset; 129 below Dominique Kieffer's house in Normandy; 130 designer Kelly Hoppen; 131 Architect Gilles Pellerin's house in Cannes; 132 Karim Rashid's New York apartment; 134 above Richard & Lucille Lewin's house in Plettenberg Bay, South Africa designed by Seth Stein; 134 below right a house in North Province, South Africa, designed by Collett-Zarzycki Architects & Designers; 135 designer Kelly Hoppen; 136 left Anthony Hudson's barn in Norfolk; 137 right designed by Emily Todhunter.

Author's acknowledgements

With many thanks to Jacqui and Kate, and fond memories of those intimate meetings with Maggie, Hilary and Nadine standing around the lightbox. Also gratitude to AWJ who runs the bath and pours the drinks when they are most needed. Happy bathtimes!